ETCHED IN GOLD

The Story of America's First-Ever Olympic Gold Medal Winning Softball Team

RON BABB

MASTERS PRESS

A Division of Howard W. Sams & Company

Published by Masters Press
A Division of Howard W. Sams & Company
2647 Waterfront Pkwy E. Dr, Suite 100, Indianapolis, IN 46214

Printed in the United States of America.

97 98 99 00 01   10 9 8 7 6 5 4 3 2 1

Library of Congress Cataloging-in-Publication Data

Babb, Ron.
   Etched in gold: the story of America's first-ever Olympic gold medal winning softball team / Ron Babb.
          p.   cm.
     ISBN 1-57028-131-9 (trade cloth)
     1. Softball teams -- United States. 2. Olympic Games (26th: 1996: Atlanta, Ga.) I. Title.
GV863.A1B23 1997   97-768
796.357'8'0973--dc21   CIP

There are thousands of individuals who have spent their lifetimes providing young athletes the opportunity to play the sport of softball. Most will never sign an endorsement contract, be quoted in the nation's daily newspapers or have an agent promoting them to corporate America, but for those who understand, they are the ones who made it all happen.

There is a distinction between those who provided the opportunities and those who benefited greatly from them. Because these individuals are for the most part nameless to the players involved, they have received little praise or thanks for their tireless efforts. Their thanks comes in the satisfaction that they provided the opportunity for young players to dream big dreams and ultimately achieve greatness in the sport.

Etched in Gold *is dedicated to those players who took full advantage of the opportunities that were provided. Players who competed on the ballfields of the world and represented the sport and the USA with dignity and class. It is also about those who provided those opportunities and helped turn the dreams of young athletes into reality.*

The book is dedicated to everyone who has dreamed of greatness or who has helped someone else achieve their goals.

This book is also dedicated to my family, wife Tomi and son and daughter David and Julia, who spent their summers in softball parks around the country listening to my endless preoccupation with the sports' Olympic debut. My dreams became their dreams, and we realized them together.

And, to our Lord Jesus Christ who has provided us with the abilities, talents, and vision to pursue and achieve impossible things.

TABLE OF CONTENTS

Credits:

Cover & Text Design: Suzanne Lincoln

In-house Editor: H.W. Kondras

Photo Imaging: Christina M. Smith & Terry Varvel

Contributing Photographers:
Doug Hoke
Bob Moreland
Robin Trimarchi/Columbus Ledger-Enquirer
Ben Van Hook/DUOMO Photography
Mike Hewitt/All Sport USA
Al Tielemans/Tielemans Photography
Arlan Flax/Alfa Photographics
1818 S. Quebec Way, #14-1, Denver, CO 80231

Acknowledgements

The author and publisher gratefully acknowledge the contributions of the many individuals who assisted in making *Etched in Gold* possible.

Front and center are the players and coaches who represented the USA so proudly throughout the entire selection process, team tour and, finally, the Olympic Games. You are all champions. Without your heart, inspiration and dedication, there would have been no reason to make the effort.

We also recognize the visionaries who made the Olympic quest their life's work and then who shared the experience with all of us. We are all encouraged and uplifted to have known you and to have caught just a brief glimpse of the vision that pushed you.

To those who contributed directly to the production of the work itself we offer our thanks including photographers Doug Hoke, Robin Trimarchi, Bob Moreland, Mike Hewitt, Ben Van Hook, Al Tielemans and Arlan Flax.

To Tom Bast of Masters Press, who shared our excitement about the project, Suzanne Lincoln, who converted mountains of text and photos into a masterful design, and Holly Kondras, who made the difficult task seem enjoyable, we offer our sincere thanks.

Etched in Gold

THE DREAM FULFILLED

Exactly 29 years, 21 days and nine hours after the birth of softball's Olympic dream, the impossible became a reality with the sport's Olympic debut at 9 a.m., July 21, 1996. No single moment in softball history was anticipated with so much excitement.

The 1996 Olympics will be remembered not only as a landmark event for the fifteen who were on the field, but also for those who played before and cleared the way. A historic bringing together of what was, what is and what will someday be in the sport of softball!

In 1991, women's fast pitch softball formally received its long awaited invitation from the International Olympic Committee to take its spot on the program of the 1996 Olympic Games. But for some it was just too late, careers and other responsibilities had cut short their playing days and their dreams of Olympic glory.

For more than three decades, the nation's top softball athletes had believed that at some point in their career they would represent the USA in the Olympics. And for more than three decades — seven consecutive summer games — they saw their hopes crumble into dust as softball was passed over.

Legendary players such as Joan Joyce, Bertha Tickey, Kathy Arendsen and a host of their teammates, hardly recognizable to the general public but all the same the dominant players of their era, were born too soon to realize their Olympic dreams. Arendsen was once quoted that her life goal was to play in the Olympics but that it was a goal "that may never be realized." Her words turned out to be prophetic upon her retirement in 1993.

The pressure of fulfilling the dreams of the previous generations of softball athletes placed a lot of pressure on the athletes who finally made it to the Olympic playing field. After all, if you wait for days... months... 29 years for anything, there is a lot of anticipated payback.

For the most part, softball managed to take the moment from expectation to realization. There are few moments in anyone's life in which such high expectations are realized. But in softball's case, the dream was not only fulfilled, but the moment was even more glorious than anyone could ever have imagined.

TOP: *Among those who made the early days memorable were Don E. Porter, ASA executive director; USA and Raybestos Brakettes head coach, Ralph Raymond; Hall of Famer Bertha Tickey and Vincent Devitt, Brakettes general manager.* Photo courtesy of National Softball Hall of Fame.

LEFT: *Players like Hall of Famers Nancy Welborn and Carol Spanks were among many outstanding softball athletes who contributed to the early success of USA Softball National teams in international competition. Pictured with hardware from the 1970 ASA Women's Major National Championship.* Photo courtesy of National Softball Hall of Fame.

CLOCKWISE FROM TOP LEFT: *Plungerhead leading the cheers; USA fans; The next generation of Olympic dreamers were there to cheer on their heroes; No shortage of good ole red, white and blue patriotism at Golden Park in Columbus, Georgia.* Photos courtesy of International Softball Federation/Bob Moreland.

There was a feeling of destiny in the air surrounding Golden Park the day of the Olympic final between China and the USA. Fans lined up at the gates hours before the contest, each sensing that they were about to witness a truly historic moment in sport.

The lines were so long that they stretched outside of the stadium grounds spilling across a large expanse of parking onto the public streets. For several miles of road at the outskirts of the stadium's gates, ticket seekers lined the avenues each armed with signs noting their pleas for tickets. Tickets for the finals were going for four times the original price but few were willing to part with their special pass to softball history.

Inside the stadium the anticipation was incredible. The media had turned out in record numbers, overflowing the tribune seating areas into public seating and completely filling an adjacent media center located across the parking lot in a newly constructed civic center complex. Even if they would have to view the moment via television monitors in the press room, the sportswriters of America could sense the story unfolding before them. It was the story of a lifetime and one too good to pass on.

The USA team found themselves on the threshold of history and driven by what they collectively sensed as their own special moment of destiny. Regardless of the accomplishments of teams of the future, they understood that they were among the original strands of the historic tapestry that would be woven with every pitch and every swing of the bat. There would be only one first USA Olympic softball team, and they were to set precedents for every team that followed.

RIGHT: *Media from around the world covered the historic event.* Photos courtesy of International Softball Federation/Bob Moreland.

The USA came into the Olympics as the favored gold medalists, some even proclaiming them as the real "Dream Team" of the Games. And why not ?— with an impressive 110-1 international record dating back to 1986 and three consecutive World Championship and Pan American Games titles to their credit. However, USA head coach Ralph Raymond cautioned that <u>champions are decided by what goes on between the lines and not by other factors</u>. The USA team knew their challenge was not only against China but against their own doubts and fears.

Bu Softball

The title game was scoreless until the third inning when Laura Berg singled to start things for the USA. Berg watched intently as teammate Dot Richardson bounced and stretched before stepping into the box to take her swings against Chinese pitcher Yaju Liu.

And, then it came, the shot that was heard around the world. Richardson hit a jolting right field rope that sent Chinese outfielder Qiang Wei scurrying to the fence in time to witness the ball slicing past her as it completed its destination into the stands and into history.

Berg and Richardson rounded the bases as the sound of a deafening chorus of "USA... USA" resonated from a raucous crowd of supporters who had waited hours, days and for some, decades to live this moment.

With arms raised in triumph they crossed the plate, Berg first, then Richardson. They were greeted by a swarming host of teammates who in an instant realized that their dreams and those of decades of softball athletes had been fulfilled.

LEFT: *A vocal crowd of supporters were on hand throughout to encourage the USA team.* Photos courtesy of International Softball Federation/Bob Moreland.

OPPOSITE PAGE: *Dr. Dot Richardson in triumphant jubilation after delivering the game winning home run in the final against China.* Photo © 1996 Robin Trimarchi

The images of the 1996 Olympic Games are as vivid today as they were the evening that the USA Softball women's team received their long awaited gold medals.

There is the image of hands raised in triumph and tears streaming down faces as America's national anthem played in the background, mingled with the cheers of joyous fans .

ABOVE: *USA gold medalists celebrate the moment. From left: Dot Richardson, Kim Maher, Lisa Fernandez, Shelly Stokes, Laura Berg, Christa Williams, Leah O'Brien, Sheila Cornell, Michele Smith, Michele Granger and Lisa Harrigan.*

Photo © 1996 Robin Trimarchi

There are the images of teammates Dot Richardson, Lisa Fernandez, Kim Maher and Michele Smith, who had each overcome their own obstacles to make it onto that field that night.

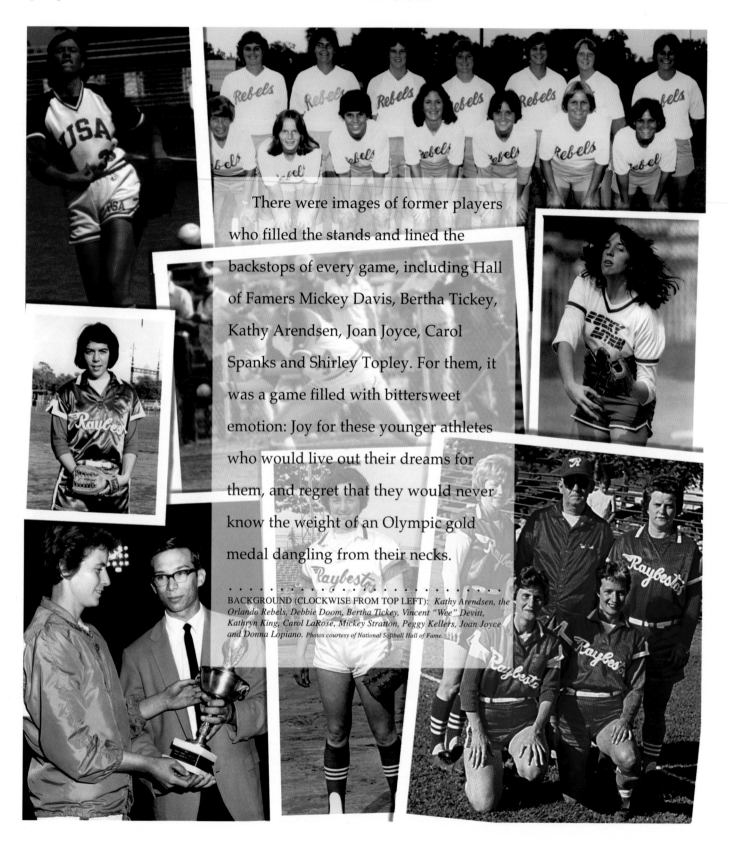

There were images of former players who filled the stands and lined the backstops of every game, including Hall of Famers Mickey Davis, Bertha Tickey, Kathy Arendsen, Joan Joyce, Carol Spanks and Shirley Topley. For them, it was a game filled with bittersweet emotion: Joy for these younger athletes who would live out their dreams for them, and regret that they would never know the weight of an Olympic gold medal dangling from their necks.

BACKGROUND (CLOCKWISE FROM TOP LEFT): *Kathy Arendsen, the Orlando Rebels, Debbie Doom, Bertha Tickey, Vincent "Wee" Devitt, Kathryn King, Carol LaRose, Mickey Stratton, Peggy Kellers, Joan Joyce and Donna Lopiano.* Photos courtesy of National Softball Hall of Fame.

Of all the images of that night, perhaps the most poignant to longtime followers of the sport was that of softball's mentor and longtime ambassador Don Porter delivering the first pitch to start the competition. The significance of this action may have been lost to most of the crowd, but to those who had participated in the work of making softball an Olympic sport, that pitch was the fulfillment of a promise made to players worldwide almost 30 years before. Don Porter had set forth on a quest to see softball recognized as an Olympic sport, and it had finally happened.

Few understood fully the price that had been paid by Porter. Realization of the dream had not been easy. Porter had faced many challenges and avoided difficult traps that were hidden at every turn along the way. There were the doubters who chided him at every step of the difficult path and attempted to convince him that his dream was ill-advised. There were profiteers and power seekers whose only visions were of their own personal gain. During these years of struggle for Olympic glory, Porter also had to face personal challenges, including a battle with a life threatening illness. But, the faces of his players had urged him on, and Porter had proven himself true to his glorious quest — Olympic softball was a reality.

Above: Don Porter and Berneta Kethan, wife of the late Bill Kethan.
Photo © 1996 Robin Trimarchi

The day was far greater than any sporting event could deliver on its own. It was a defining moment for the millions who had cherished the dream through its more than three decades of pursuit, a triumph of the human spirit and a tribute to the thousands who would not let the dream die.

The dream fulfilled, the story of the amazing journey to the gold remains untold to most. It has been a journey that has stretched around the world and enlisted thousands of players, fans and volunteers along the way, all sharing the same vision of providing the finest softball athletes in the world the opportunity to be Olympians. *Etched in Gold* is a tribute to America's first-ever Olympic gold medal winning softball team and the people who helped make it happen.

ABOVE: *USA's 18-year-old pitcher Christa Williams made her Olympic and NBC debut*. TOP RIGHT: *National media attention reached an all-time high at the Games. Pictured - USA pitcher Michele Smith. Photos courtesy of International Softball Federation/Bob Moreland* BOTTOM RIGHT: *Hall of Famer Diane Schumacher fulfills a dream of her own by delivering a first pitch during the Olympics. Photo © 1996 Robin Trimarchi* OPPOSITE PAGE: *Capacity crowds. Photo courtesy of International Softball Federation/Bob Moreland*

ER

…mber 1988

ASA Council Members

Don Porter, Executive Director

Olympic Status for Softball

…t of you are aware the Olympic Games are presently going on in Seoul. In
…ion, the International Olympic Committee (IOC) held its General Session just
…to the start of the Games.

…president (Bert …
…ded the IOC meeti… the
…l sport on the Oly…

…many know and tho…
… ten years to brin…
…y course and has … that
…contend with the w…

…have been assured …rage-
…ftball would in tim… best
…C, in
… have most recen… agreed
…nt of the IOC, in p… …xt IOC
…oute to gain Olympi…
…ts infinite wisdom,
…o reconsider softba…
…Session in Calgary (
…were informed the d…
…Seoul (September 198…

…During the IOC Sessi…
…before the Session
…support of softball
…Barcelona (1992) h…
…program. Since the…
…it was agreed that
…August 1989. A dec…

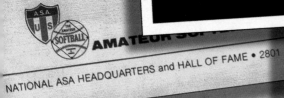

AMATEUR SOF…

NATIONAL ASA HEADQUARTERS and HALL OF FAME • 2801 …

…ne meantime, the only door left open for 1992 is th…
…g an exhibition sport in Barcelona. We have subm…
…n's softball and hope to hear something around the e…

…e this has been most frustrating to many of us,
…support from IOC members during the Session
…ranch's words during my meeting with him at Seoul;
…baseball 25 years to get in." Our response to Pre
…ave not been at it 25 years, it seems like it!"

…e the delay on softball's acceptance is disappoin
…end of the game, we must go on to strengthen a
…ams and organization and help when and where
…lopment of the sport both domestically and internati

…big disappointment is for the athletes who are
…rience and the recognition a sport receives in atta
…f President Vecke Andy Loechner Bill Keth

Barcelona, 15 september 1989

Dear Don,

I am very glad to confirm you what yesterday the …
…nate officially the SOFTBALL how EXHIBITION S…
Congratulations for all Softball Family.
Very best wishes.

Miquel Ortín.

COMITÉ INTERNATIONAL OLYMP…
CHATEAU DE VIDY 1007 LAUSANNE SUISSE

Mr. Don E. PORTER,
President,
International Softball Federati…
2801 N.E. 50th Street,
OKLAHOMA CITY, OK 73…
U.S.A.

Lausanne, 10th Janua…
Ref. No.   112…

Re : Softball

Dear Mr. Porter,

    May I acknowledge receipt of your letter of 14t…
comments of which I have duly noted.

    I understand your disappointment regarding th…
Board's decision to eliminate exhibition sports at th…
XXVth Olympiad to be held in Barcelona.

    However, I hope that you will understand that it …
add more sports to the programme of the Barcelona Game…
have twenty five official and 3 exhibition sports.

                                    Yours sincer…

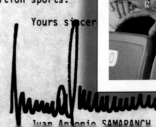

Juan Antonio SAMARANCH

CASE POSTALE 356, 1001 LAUSANNE

Ø 25 32 71/72/73 ▣ 454 024 CH FAX 021 24 15 52 ✆ CIO

BANQUE: UNION DE BANQUES SUISSES CH. POST.

Mr. Don E. PORTER
President
Fédération Internationale de Soft
P.O. Box 11437
2801 N.E. 50th Street
OKLAHOMA CITY / Oklahoma 731
United States

Birmingham, 16th June 1991
Ref. no.   2851   /91/jsb

e : Games of the XXVI Olympiad, Atlanta 1996

ear Mr. Porter,

Following the meeting of the 97th IOC Session here in Birminghar
ve pleasure in informing you that it has been decided, in agreement
th the Atlanta Committee for the Olympic Games, to add women's sof
the programme of the Games of the XXVI Olympiad, Atlanta 1996.

The softball tournament will comprise 8 teams.

This decision has been taken on an exceptional basis, for the Gar
the XXVI Olympiad only, due to softball's popularity in the United
tes. Final arrangements for the tournament are to be discussed
ween the IOC, your Federation and the Atlanta Committee for the
mpic Games. I am of course at your disposal for any further
rmation in this respect.

Yours sincerely,

tion sport   in Barcelona.

l and hope to hear something around the end of October.

of us, we were encouraged by the

2

FROM
DREAM
TO
REALITY

There were a lot of well-wishers and dreamers during softball's early days as an Olympic hopeful, but the man who caught the vision and made it his lifetime quest was Don Porter.

Porter was just a young man when talk about the idea began to become commonplace in softball circles. He knew that more than talk was needed to make the dream a reality. But he did not realize how much frustration lay ahead for him and his sport. Those who know him best understand that just as the Olympics became a defining point for softball, it was one for Porter as well.

The elusive dream began almost 30 years ago in Stratford, Connecticut when representatives from Canada, Japan, Australia and the USA met and became united in their feelings that women's fast pitch indeed had a bright future internationally. Later, teams from Australia, Japan, New Zealand, New Guinea and the USA met in the first Women's World Championship in 1965 in Melbourne and the long journey to Olympic recognition was in motion.

One of Porter's first recollections of his attempt to gain Olympic recognition for the sport came in 1968 at the Olympic Games in Mexico City. The late Avery Brundage, an American and then president of the International Olympic Committee (IOC), carved out a moment to meet with Porter in his hotel suite concerning softball's future as an Olympic sport. "Young man, softball is a great American pastime. I played it myself in Chicago, but it has a long way to go to make the program of the Olympics," Brundage said. "You must develop it as more than an American sport and you must have patience."

Brundage, although cordial, was never strongly supportive of softball's efforts. He reportedly had an open bias against team sports in general, believing they encouraged nationalistic feelings among its participants. However, their brief discussion did give Porter some important information that would be needed to take softball forward in its Olympic pursuit: Someone would have

to take the sport to the international level if the dream was ever to become a reality.

Softball began to show progress under the International Softball Federation's (ISF) developing World Championship structure. Successful world events had already been completed in Australia (1965) and 1966 in

RIGHT: *Don Porter in Lausanne.*

OPPOSITE PAGE: *Don Porter, the quest begins.*

Photos courtesy of International Softball Federation

Mexico City. However, despite its success, the first women's world championship featured only five nations, not even close to the type of involvement that would be required for an invitation to the Olympics.

Over the next decade, Porter parlayed his position as the executive director of the Amateur Softball Association (ASA) and secretary-general of the ISF into a power structure that vaulted him into leadership not only in the United States, but internationally as well. With each passing year, it was clear that Porter was emerging as the driving force behind softball's Olympic movement.

As softball was growing rapidly in America under Porter's direction, the sport was also beginning to take its first steps internationally. Softball's Olympic mission was beginning to take form as nation upon nation opened their doors to Porter and his sport.

In America, Porter had taken the ASA from under 20,000 registered teams nationally in 1965 to over 275,000 teams by 1991, the year of softball's Olympic announcement. ASA programs were developing rapidly including a large umpire base that included some 60,000 registered officials, making it one of the largest officiating organizations in the world.

The growth of the sport in the USA provided an enormous technical support base that Porter and the ASA used to develop programs around the world. In the early years, the ASA not only introduced the sport to a country, but they typically provided the early nurturing as well. It was not unusual for the ASA to provide not only technical advice and encouragement, but nuts-and-bolts training for coaches, players and umpires. More often than not, the ASA supplied the fledgling new programs with even their first supply of bats, balls and other essential equipment.

All the while Porter was leading softball's conquest, personally logging more than 200,000 travel miles per year. Porter knew, however, that his strength lay in the support of leaders within the ASA including a long succession of presidents. Porter was the first to recognize that the success of softball's Olympic

ASA Team and Umpire Registrations from 1964 to 1996

Year	Adult Teams	Youth Teams	Total Teams	Adult Umpires	Youth Umpires	Total Umpires	Total Registrations
1964	15,195	—	15,195	6,987	—	6,987	22,182
1966	17,636	—	17,636	7,790	—	7,790	25,426
1968	21,732	—	21,732	9,359	—	9,359	31,091
1970	29,075	—	29,075	12,168	—	12,168	41,243
1972	42,101	—	42,101	17,252	—	17,252	59,353
1974	55,617	6,207	61,824	24,947	—	24,947	86,771
1976	72,503	10,025	82,528	34,051	—	34,051	116,579
1978	91,724	14,299	106,023	41,512	—	41,512	147,535
1980	110,012	17,779	127,791	50,948	—	50,948	178,739
1982	133,133	22,386	155,519	61,013	730	61,743	217,262
1984	146,224	28,680	174,904	61,873	1,087	62,960	237,864
1986	167,577	35,188	202,765	59,726	1,135	60,861	263,626
1988	181,591	39,867	221,458	56,362	1,179	57,541	278,999
1990	187,945	45,982	233,927	55,140	1,450	56,590	290,517
1992	202,132	56,999	259,131	57,582	1,886	59,468	318,599
1994	196,089	67,520	263,609	54,656	2,057	56,713	320,322
1996	183,492	78,639	262,131	51,983	2,234	54,217	316,348

Important dates:

1965 — Beginning of the push for softball as an Olympic sport

1974 —Start of the ASA youth program

1991 — Softball is admitted as an Olympic sport for 1996

movement was directly tied to the support of leaders such as Bill Kethan, Texas; George Cron, New Jersey; Fred Blum, New York; John Nagy, Ohio; Joe Barber, Connecticut; Andy Pendergast, Washington; Howard Honaker, Ohio; Red Halpern, Idaho; Chuck McCord, Illinois; Andy Loechner, Pennsylvania; Bert Weeks, North Carolina; Bill Smith, Nebraska; Jack Aaron, Texas and Wayne Myers, Indiana. These individuals passed the Olympic baton from one year to the next never losing site of the ultimate goal.

It would be difficult to calculate the ASA's financial investment in the process, let us just say that it was substantial. Not only was the program sending its best around the world, it was also developing the USA's competitive contingent as well. The ASA certainly had a vested interest in developing the programs of the world, but not in detriment to its own national team program.

In fact, in the two decades preceeding the sport's Olympic announcement, the ASA underwent unprecedent growth, particularly in its youth developmental programs. The ASA was the only softball organization pouring millions into an investment in the sport's youth, pledging that the next generation of USA Softball players would be better than the one that proceeded it.

That dedication created a youth program that grew over 1,000 percent in its first 20 years. Before Title IX opened any doors, the ASA was investing big time dollars and hours into creating competitive opportunities for young women. The investment has paid off by producing the finest softball players in the world and over 78,000 youth teams each year, over 95 percent of which are female. In a recent survey conducted among NCAA Division I softball programs, 80 percent of all the players now playing in college were recruited directly from ASA programs.

In the early years, Kethan and Porter were joined internationally by Mexico's Jose Anzorena; Puerto Rico's Ismael Delgado; Canada's Bob Van Impe; Japan's Jiro Iwano and Dr. Tatsuo Ohura; Philippine Governor Isidro Rodriquez, Letty Paguia and Bert Landero; Taiwan's Ho Ming Chang;

Australia's Esther Deason and Merle Short; New Zealand's John Voyle, George Vincent, Alf Whelan and Ray Weaver and Luis Mejia of the Dominican Republic.

The ISF family began to grow following the completion of successful world championships in the 1960's and '70's encouraging leaders and supporters to come forth including Jan Crafford, South Africa; Theo Vleeshhouwer, Netherlands; Clovis Lodewijks, Netherland Antilles; Meliton Sanchez, Panama; Malcolm Burne, Zimbawe and Steven Huang, Chinese Taipei.

As the developmental side of the mission was progressing, Porter began to turn up the heat politically. It was not enough to meet the IOC charter requirements; he knew he would also have to convince those who had the votes that softball was worthy.

In the early days it was almost impossible to get a meeting with a voting IOC member. "I remember getting on an elevator in a hotel in which an IOC meeting was being held and riding up and down until someone from the IOC got on. I used this brief time to lobby for softball. After they got off the elevator, I stayed on and waited for the next IOC member to get on. I was determined to do whatever it takes to get softball on the program," Porter said. No hotel lobby, restaurant or elevator was safe from Porter's relentless campaigning.

Porter's approach was active, but not overbearing. "There were lots of people seeking the IOC member's time, and I saw a lot of mistakes being made along the way. I didn't want to create a situation where an IOC member would want to avoid me because they knew I was always pressing them. So, I did some homework and got to know what their interests were so that when I met them I could talk about their interests also. After they talked about their interests, they would usually give me a few minutes to talk about mine. I had great empathy and respect for their position," Porter said.

Porter was among the most disciplined and active of any sport leaders and never missed an IOC meeting in almost three decades of attendance.

Despite Porter's patience, the years leading to the decision to make softball an Olympic sport were filled with difficult, frustrating and even life threatening moments. Even through the frustrations, it was a dream, although elusive at times, that was pursued with such ardor that everyone closely involved knew that one day it would come true. Yes was the only acceptable answer.

Much was accomplished in pursuit of the dream. The sport blossomed internationally to include 80 countries by 1991, and over 100 nations by the Olympics in 1996. A new generation of fans began to seek out and follow the sport as it emerged from the ballfields of the United States to the parks of literally every country in the world. World competitions such as the Pan American, Asian, South Pacific, Southeast Asian, Central-American, Caribbean and Central American Games proved an excellent exhibition arena for a sport whose best days were still to come. Dozens of regional and continental championships and hundreds of team exchanges and technical and

equipment support programs began to spring up from continent to continent, bolstering the efforts of each country who wanted to get on board the softball express.

The IOC, before current president Juan Antonio Samaranch, was not well organized and communication was often slow or non-existent. Porter's work was complicated by the fact that there appeared to be no consistent formula for getting a sport on the program. "It was difficult trying to even identify the decision makers. We would pursue individuals only to find out that they had no authority to

help us. The early days were filled with roadblocks," Porter said.

Porter pursued every possibility in attempting to get the attention of the IOC including personally writing "thousands" of letters, most of which were never answered. In the meanwhile, Porter continued his work to prepare the competitive side of his sport. As the years passed, softball's resume began to become more and more impressive as the number of completed international championships and the number of participating countries continued to grow.

"We were running an on-going tally sheet and attempting to impress the IOC with our mounting successes," Porter said.

Communication with the IOC improved dramatically with Samaranch's assumption of the presidency in 1981. Although Samaranch's counsel to Porter continued to be "patience," the path to the Olympics seemed to be more tangible and reachable. However, obstacles continued to present themselves.

The International Softball Federation (ISF) was in the process of organizing its

third women's world championship and had awarded the event to Taiwan. Somehow in the process of organizing a softball tournament, the championship became embroiled in the international politics and problems that were surfacing in that region of the world in the early 1980's.

China was beginning to move its international policy away from years of isolationism and had expressed interest in the ISF's attempts to recruit them to its membership. Six months prior to the 1982 ISF Women's World Championship, China had made overtures to Porter that they were in fact planning to make the trip to Taiwan. This would have set a political precedent as the first time China had sent an official delegation of any type to participate in an event held in Taiwan. However, China's interest proved to be more political postering than genuine interest in the sport.

China, seemingly feeling that they could leverage their team's attendance in the event effectively against Taiwan, began to pick away at the tournament's structure. Their first complaint was the proposed use of Taiwan's national flag and anthem at the event. China maintained that Taiwan was not a nation and therefore the flag and anthem were inappropriate and an insult to them. Taiwan defiantly objected, arguing that Taiwan was indeed separated from China and they

---

Thursday, October 4, 1979

Softball Czar Tries To End China Conflict

By BOB BONEBRAKE

OKLAHOMA CITY (AP) — Next time a dispute arises between two world powers, the U.N. might do well to call in Don Porter to practice a little of his sport diplomacy.

Say a border war crops up between two countries. The Oklahoma City resident might fly in, flip a coin to see which country gets first bats and referee a lively international softball game — winner take all.

"I think the main benefit to any government in participating in sports on an international level is that it promotes communication between countries," Porter said. "You can bring countries that really don't have anything else in common together through sports."

Porter, the secretary general of the International Softball Federation headquartered here, got a chance to prove his theories recently when he got mainland China to agree to play softball with Taiwan.

HE RETURNED OVER the weekend from a lengthy trip promoting softball, which kept him in Communist China for 15 days.

"We made some real progress," he said. "We got the Chinese to agree to join our federation, without the requirement Taiwan be ousted. From all I can determine this is the first international group they have agreed to join without that stipulation."

Porter's next move is to meet with Taiwanese officials later this month to get them to agree to continue their long association with the ASA.

"Its going to be sensitive," he said. "But it is worth working for. Since the Chinese didn't put any real stipulations on their membership I think it can be worked out. The possibilities are tremendous."

One of those tremendous possibilities is that the first government sanctioned group of Communist Chinese athletes may be making a trip to the tiny island nation they have long refused to recognize.

"WE COULD BE getting the two together soon," he said. "Our 1982 world championships are scheduled to be held in Taipei and I believe Peking wants to enter a team.

"Things are really changing over there. Before they wouldn't even talk to us."

Porter has had success, but sports and politics don't always mix that smoothly.

For years the International Olympic Committee has had only limited success getting countries to forget their international disagreements. The most tragic failure ended with the deaths of several Israeli athletes in a terrorism incident at the games in Munich, Germany.

"I guess I am as proud of this country as anyone," Porter said. "But, the only way I can see to cut down on the political blocks to international competition is to play down the nationalism angle.

"WE ARE PLAYING down nationalism. We're not letting teams fly their flag and not playing national anthems for the winners," he said. "We are trying to make it athlete against athlete and not country against country."

were totally within their rights as a free nation.

Of course, China's challenge was not really about the flag and anthem of Taiwan. Their challenge was ultimately against Taiwan's right to exist, which was China's real objection to the tournament's location. Taiwan's persistence in calling themselves the Republic of China (ROC) continued to irritate and inflame the Chinese, who maintained that there was only one China and that they were the only representative that should be allowed in the event.

The problem was compounded by the fact that Porter, an American, was viewed warily by Chinese officials who at one point were convinced that he was not only speaking for softball, but the U.S. State Department as well. Nothing could have been further from the truth. Porter's only mission was to further the sport and conduct a world championship. The political issues that China persistently raised were not appropriate within a sports context that had gone to great ends to limit that type of influence.

The political issues persisted and Porter became a less than willing spokesperson for not only his sport, but U.S. foreign policy as well. While the China/Taiwan issue was being argued at the United Nations, softball had unwittingly been pulled into the fray and Porter in the six months leading up to the event became a target of public review. At the height of the

Deadline Set for China, Taiwan to Settle Dispute

The secretary general of the International Softball Federation said Tuesday a March 15 deadline had been set for China and Taiwan to work out the problems that are besetting a proposed tournament on Taiwan.

If a compromise isn't reached by the deadline, Don Porter said, "we will look at moving" the Fifth Women's World Softball Tournament scheduled for Taipei July 2-11.

Porter said that the problems were caused by "politics pure and simple" and that "Taiwan is just as guilty as China in bringing these problems in. We are trying to reach a compromise, but frankly it doesn't look too promising.

"Both sides are trying to gain as much politically out of this as they can, and softball is in the middle."

At issue is Taiwan's insistence on raising the Taiwanese flag and playing the Taiwanese national anthem at the opening and closing ceremonies. China maintains that Taiwan is not a country, but a province of China, and therefore does not possess either a national flag or national anthem.

China's official Xinhua news agency quoted an official of the Chinese Softball Association as saying Tuesday "some Americans" in the ISF were creating conditions unacceptable for China to participate in the tournament in Taipei.

"We have noticed that recently some Americans in the ISF, ignoring the resolution of the ISF congress, take a part of the Chinese territory as an independent state, and have used this as an excuse to proclaim that organizers of the upcoming championships could use Taiwan's so-called 'national flag' and 'national anthem' at the opening and closing ceremonies.

"This undisguised attempt to create 'two Chinas' is absolutely impermissible," the unidentified spokesman was quoted by Xinhua as saying.

"We don't care if there are two Chinas or four Chinas, and we have explained that in Telexes to China," Porter said. "We are trying to put on a softball tournament, and we are caught in the middle of a political battle."

He said he had received several cables from China "in which they outlined their position," but said the ISF "also has received cables from the other side, too."

"There are two things here," Porter said. "One is political and the other is softball. We're trying to separate the two. We are interested only in softball. We just want to put on a good tournament where the kids can come and have a good time."

Even though China has opposed the use of the Taiwanese flag and anthem, it has said repeatedly in the past it stands ready to send a team to Taiwan.

If a Chinese team did go to Taiwan, it would be the first delegation from the mainland since the communists drove the Chinese nationalists out to Taiwan in 1949. China now is trying to persuade Taiwan to reunite with the mainland, an effort it says is hampered by U.S. arms sales to the island.

A softball delegation from Taiwan left Oklahoma City for home on Tuesday after meeting with Porter for two days. He said the March 15 deadline was set at those meetings.

By The Associated Press

problem, Porter participated in meetings with IOC President Samaranch in Taiwan and Hong Kong. Samaranch related concern that the problems could have an adverse affect on the

Taiwan to accept China in tourney

TAIPEI, Taiwan (AP) — Taiwan, putting aside political differences with the People's Republic of China, will formally accept China's participation in the Fifth World Women's Softball Championships in July, officials announced today.

Chinese sports officials already have said mainland China would participate in the Taiwan tournament. There was no immediate response, however, to today's announcement.

A spokesman for China's State Sports Federation said he had no comment until the nation was directly notified by the International Softball Federation.

Oklahoma Cityan Don Porter, secretary general of the ISF, said all 46 ISF members, including China, will be informed within three days of the decision to hold the meet in Taiwan.

Taiwan, however, will not send invitations directly to Peking.

Don Porter

Porter made the announcement at a news conference at Taipei's Grand Hotel after four days of discussions with Ho Ming-Chang, president of the Chinese-Taipei Softball Association, and other sports officials here.

He said ISF members were required to submit their responses within 15 days of receiving invitations. The softball championships will be July 2-11.

It would mark the first time athletes from mainland China would compete in a sports event in Taiwan, seat of the rival Nationalist Chinese government, since the Communist government was established in Peking in 1949.

Softball

Taiwan will allow its rival mainland China to participate in the fifth World Women's Softball Championships to be held in Taiwan July 2-11, Don Porter, secretary general of the International Softball Federation (ISF), said Tuesday. Porter made the announcement after he and Ho Ming-Chang, president of Taiwan's Chinese-Taipei Softball Association, concluded their four days of talks. They signed an agreement that Taiwan formally will host the July tourney in Taipei and that all of 46 ISF members, including Peking, will be invited. It will be the first time Taiwan officially has approved a visit from any citizens of mainland China since the communists took over the mainland from the Nationalists in 1949 following a four-year civil war. Porter told a news conference before leaving for his home in Oklahoma City that it had also been agreed Taiwan would send formal invitation to Peking through the ISF.

Olympic community as well. Samaranch knew that China's announced plans to re-enter the Olympics could also gravitate into similar destructive issues for his movement in the future.

After the discussions, Samaranch advised Porter that perhaps the best solution would be to move the championship to Rome. This was a difficult situation for Porter. The IOC's most influential representative was asking him to choose the road of least resistance, while at the same time the ISF membership was beginning to line-up in support of Taiwan.

Whatever the decision, the potential ramifications were disturbing. Porter greatly valued the counsel of Samaranch and understood totally that his support could be of great value in getting softball on the Olympic program. But he had strong feelings of loyalty to Taiwan because of its

RIGHT: *Don Porter following press conference in Hong Kong Airport.*
Photo courtesy of International Softball Federation

support of softball during its important early years of development internationally.

The problems were out on the table for everyone's consumption due largely to the major media coverage the situation illicited worldwide.

Porter was besiged by media from around the world at his headquarters office in Oklahoma City. Upon his arrival in Hong Kong to meet with Samaranch, he was met by over a hundred journalists at the airport. "Cameras were everywhere. I could barely move through the airport. Finally, I was directed into a meeting room at the airport where we held an impromptu press conference. The room was so jammed with reporters that it was hard to breathe. It was a scary situation to walk into," Porter said.

It got scarier. After the ISF had made its decision to support Taiwan and China had declined an appearance at the event, the public openly began to divide ranks and Porter became the center of protest. Porter had wanted only to promote his sport and conduct a successful world championship. Now he would have to continue to deal with political issues that threatened to derail the progress he had made in promoting the sport over the last decade.

The event went on and was attended by 23 nations, the largest field ever at a world event. The climate of the event, however, was beginning to weigh on Porter, who by

Hopes Fading for Chinese Softball Trip to Taiwan

By MICHAEL PARKS, *Times Staff Writer*

PEKING—China's hopes of sending a women's softball team to Taiwan in July, the first such contact in more than three decades, appear to be fading because of a dispute over whether Taiwan will raise the Chinese Nationalist flag as host of the women's world softball championship.

Peking said Wednesday, after a month of behind-the-scenes negotiations, that if the Nationalist flag is raised and the Nationalist anthem is played, as the International Softball Federation has agreed, its team will not participate in the games.

The federation decision, the Communist Party newspaper People's Daily said, is "a vicious attempt to create 'two Chinas,' thus barring the Chinese national women's softball team from going to Taipei for the championships."

"The 1 billion Chinese will say no to this," the People's Daily declared, dismissing various federation attempts at a compromise.

A similar commentary in the newspaper Sports News added that

Taiwan "is not a country but a part of China's territory. There can be no question of 'national' flag and 'national' anthem at all," the paper said.

A spokesman for the Chinese Softball Assn. told the official New China News Agency that the players are eager to go to Taiwan for the championships, but that it is "entirely out of the question" if the Chinese Nationalist flag and anthem are used.

He added that the association has not yet received an official invitation to participate, thus sparing it the need for an immediate decision, and is continuing to seek a resolution of the question through the International Softball Federation, though with apparently diminishing hope.

The prospect of sending an athletic team to Taiwan has excited imaginations here, for it would be the first organized contact with the island since the Chinese Nationalists retreated from the mainland in 1949 after their loss to the Commu-nis...

Softball Diplomacy and the Two Chinas

HONG KONG—Not so long ago, it appeared that "softball diplomacy" might follow the path of Ping-Pong, with ostensibly innocuous sports contests paving the way for talks between two avowed enemies.

In 1971 a table-tennis exchange signaled negotiations between the U.S. and China, after 20-odd years of mutual recrimination and a bloody war. This year it seemed a

Asia

by Robert Keatley

women's softball tournament could do the same for China and Taiwan, where rival regimes continue to wage (at least verbally) a civil war most people think was settled in 1949.

The fifth World Women's Softball Championship, sponsored by a 40-member federation, is to be held in Taipei this July. Invitations were sent to all members, including China (which joined soon after the Taiwan delegation was downgraded from representing the "Republic of China" to becoming the "Chinese Taipei Softball Association").

Soon came trouble. The Nationalists sent out invitation telegrams stating the venue as Taipei, Taiwan Province, the Republic of China. Foul ball, cried Peking. There is only one China and the People's Republic is it—the offending telegrams must be declared "null and void." Taiwan's determination to play the Nationalist anthem and fly the Nationalist flag also were denounced. Only the Communist flag and anthem should be used—if any national symbols are needed—because Taiwan is merely a Chinese province gone astray and not an independent country.

The whole thing is an "elaborately planned . . . political trick" to create two Chinas where one is quite enough, maintains the Communist side. Moreover, it says the hapless softball association is part of the plot—"closely connected with the

longstanding U.S. plan of selling arms to Taiwan . . . and (to) brazenly create two Chinas." Sputtering retorts by softball officials that they don't care whether there are two Chinas, or four, that they merely want to organize some ballgames, earn no sympathy in Peking. Neither do official U.S. statements that it is "neutral" in the matter. Peking contends there can be no neutrality between right and wrong.

If the mainland team doesn't visit Taipei, Peking will have demonstrated again that it can stick to its principles. But the cost would be great. The games offer Peking the first real chance to send any delegation to Taiwan after years of trying. That would set an important precedent and other visits could follow, perhaps some concerned with more serious matters than base hits and strikeouts.

It appears China is letting strategy fall for the sake of petty details that it could ignore. Yet Peking has reasons for this obdurate stand.

One is to ensure that the U.S. gets the message—namely, that in the long term Peking won't tolerate a divided China and fights anything that prolongs Taiwan's separate existence. There are also internal Chinese pressures at work.

Under the guidance of Communist Party Vice Chairman Deng Xiaoping, China is modernizing its economy and government. This includes rejecting old Maoist policies and firing many thousands of bureaucrats. Moreover, it means importing (often inadvertently) foreign people and foreign ways into a China that once was closed. Many Chinese see a breakdown of morality, with crime, corruption and what passes for loose living on the rise. Others think the new policies are ideologically wrong. Those who may be fired from party or government jobs are unhappy. Thus Mr. Deng and his colleagues can't risk seeming soft on Taiwan; that might give opponents a convenient issue that could interfere with crucial economic plans.

In any case, the elderly men who run

China want to resolve the Taiwan question in their lifetimes, and they have little lifetime left. They also may believe their equally old counterparts in Taipei represent a last chance for unification. Those old Nationalists share a one-China ideal for a different China, of course) and might talk if terms are right. Their successors, however, including the native Taiwanese, oppose anything that risks loss of existing economic and political freedoms. This gives extra cause for a hard push today; tomorrow could be too late.

Ronald Reagan probably added to the dispute. His loose talk about "upgrading" U.S. relations with Taiwan and his dithering over advanced-weapons sales must seem a doublecross in Peking. After years of U.S. motion (however limited) on Taiwan, the Reagan administration appeared to put policy into reverse, as China sees it.

Finally, if Peking worries about Taiwan's next generation, it must worry even more about its own future leaders. Those who fought the civil war are dying off; or, presumably, have great concern about an offshore province that was always peripheral to mainland life. Those who have come to maturity since 1949 could well let the issue slide once they exercise power; the mainland's own development almost certainly will seem more important. Therefore, suggest some Chinese, the current campaign—whether about aircraft, softball or whatever—is designed to create a legacy. It's to ensure the issue isn't forgotten as years pass.

But nothing will bring island and mainland together. if the Taiwanese are opposed; it would be politically impossible for any U.S. administration to "abandon" Taiwan, or force a merger. Peking's best line could well be to speak softly, send those ballplayers to Taipei and hope this helps build trust where now there is suspicion.

Mr. Keatley is editor of The Asian Wall Street Journal.

Porter Here for Softball Talks

About 25 foreign teams are expected to participate in the Fifth Women's Softball Championship here in July, Don Porter, secretary general of the International Softball Federation (ISF), told reporters upon his arrival from Hongkong yesterday afternoon.

He said he had received cable and telex replies from 31 ISF affiliated member associations or federations, of which 15 indicated that they would send teams to the Taipei summer games, while 16 others either said they would not come, or have not yet decided.

Porter arrived here after attending a preparatory meeting in the British colony designed to reorganize the Amateur Softball Association of Asia (ASAA) which has been inactive since 1974. The meeting, organized by the Japan Softball Association, reportedly broke down after four hours of talks due to a split in opinions and differences among ASAA member nations.

He said that he would meet with softball leaders here to further discuss some unsettled problems and work out details for the forth-

coming world tournament. He did not elaborate.

The ISF top executive told newsmen at the CKS International Airport that he was authorized by ISF President William Kathen and the world softball body's executive council to solve, prior to his departure, problems full of political implications. He did not spell out what those problems were.

Porter pointed out that he originally did not plan to come to Taipei. He changed his mind in order to help dispose of the political dispute between the host country and especially Mainla... was admitted t... year.

The Republic o... bidding, against S... host the world tou...

Porter dodged ... regarding the ... whether or not to ... Taipei interna... However, he said ... body wrote him ... hoisting of the ho... would affect its de...

U.S. team. The United States, the world's defending champion, has not yet registered for participation.

Asked who the 15 members were that indicated they would take part, Porter replied that he could not remember.

Thomas Hsueh, who also returned to Taipei yesterday afternoon after the ASAA talk, was not satisfied with Porter's answer to the last question.

A member of the world tourney's organizing committee, Hsueh attended the Hongkong meetin... on behalf of Ho Ming-... the Chines...

Thomas Hsueh (left), representative of the ... Taipei Softball Association, returned to Taipei ye... afternoon after attending a two-day reorganizing m... of the dormant ASAA in Hongkong. Also arriving ... him was Don Porter, secretary general of the ISF.
(CNA Photo)

THE WALL STREET JOURNAL,
Monday, March 15, 1982

INTERNATIONAL

What Chinese Need Is a Good Umpire To Settle Squabble

* * *

Peking Crying Foul at Plan By Taiwan to Fly Its Flag At World Baseball Meet

By FRANK CHING
Staff Reporter of THE WALL STREET JOURNAL

PEKING—Almost three months before their athletes are to meet each other in Taiwan, the authorities in mainland China and Taiwan are engaged in a slugfest that could knock the International Women's Softball Championship out of the ballpark.

Both China and Taiwan have a stake in seeing the games proceed as scheduled July 2 to 11. Hosting an international sporting event would be a victory for Taiwan, because the island is diplomatically isolated.

And for Peking, the dispatching of a softball team to Taiwan would mark a breakthrough in Chinese attempts to establish people-to-people relations with their separated brethren across the Taiwan Straits.

The Chinese Nationalists who rule Taiwan were reluctant from the start to invite the Peking players, given their policy of shunning all contact with their archrivals and spurning all overtures for peaceful reunification with the Chinese Communists. Taiwan fears that any contact could lead to its political incorporation into the mainland.

But after International Softball Federation officials told Taiwan that to withhold an invitation to Peking wouldn't be cricket and would violate federation rules, the Taiwanese relented.

But while Taiwan had to bow to federation rules, it found some other rules more to its liking. Taiwan claimed the right, as the host country, to fly its national flag and play its national anthem at the games' opening ceremony.

The Chinese called foul. Tiyubao, the Chinese sports newspaper, declared that Taiwan "is not a country at all but part of

China's territory. There can be no question at all of a 'national' flag or 'national' anthem."

People's Daily, the official newspaper, said that if any flag were to be flown or anthem sung, "naturally they ought to be (those) of the People's Republic of China, (the host country, instead of Taiwan, a province of China."

The federation was caught in the middle. China criticized "some Americans" in the federation for "a vicious attempt to create 'two Chinas.'"

"That's a very inappropriate statement because it is totally untrue," said Don Porter, the federation's secretary general, reached by telephone in Los Angeles.

There is a distinct possibility that the games may either be postponed or moved elsewhere in view of the deadlock. Mr. Porter says that unless the two Chinese sides reach a compromise soon, the championships may be moved from Taiwan.

Even if the flag-anthem issue is resolved, another problem looms. Taiwan presumably would require all Chinese athletes to apply for visas, which China might see as recognition of Taiwan's sovereignty.

OBSERVER'S SPORTS

On Peking-Taipei 'softball cold-war'
ISF breaks Olympic rules in Taiwan case,
says I.O.C. chief

Peking, (AP) – The president of the International Olympic Committee (IOC) Juan Antonio Samaranch, indicated Wednesday the International Softball Federation (IST) is violating IOC rules by allowing Taiwan to fly its flag and play its anthem at a tournament this summer.

Samaranch also told the Associated Press in an interview that if the problem is not solved, the IOC Executive Board would take up the issue at a meeting in Rome in late May.

He indicated the ISF could be jeopardizing its own recognition by the IOC through its handling of the women's softball cham- pionships scheduled for July in Taiwan.

"First, we of the International Olympic Committee respect the independence of the International Softball Federation," Samaranch said. "But second, if ISF wants to be recognized by the IOC they have to follow the IOC rules."

The IOC forbids Taiwan's use of the nationalist "Republic of China" flag and anthem at Olympic events. The ISF, however, has agreed that Taiwan may use the nationalist flag and anthem at ceremonies this summer.

China has protested, saying Taiwan is a province of China without a national flag. It calls the ISF decision a violation of

'Yes'

He said Chinese sports officials explained the problem but did not say they would boycott the tournament. China currently is urging ISF members not to attend unless the ISF and Taiwan back down on the flag and anthem issue.

Samaranch replied "yes" when asked whether the ISF was not in accordance with IOC rules.

Samaranch said, however, China has not asked him to mediate or speak to Porter in Hong Kong.

Asked if he supported China's position in the dispute, he said, "I have to support the agreement and rules of the International Olympic Committee."

In 1979 the IOC admitted the People's Republic of China And ruled

China Not Among Entries for Softball Tourney

What was termed the largest field ever to participate in an international softball tournament was announced Wednesday, but China was not among the countries that will send a team to Taiwan this summer.

Japan, which Taiwan last week said had been rejected on technical grounds, was on the list.

In Oklahoma City, Don Porter, secretary genereal of the International Softball Federation, said 23 countries had formally accepted invitations to the Fifth

Women's World softball tournament scheduled for Taipei July 2-11.

The official entry list as listed by Porter was:

Argentina, Australia, the Bahamas, Belgium, Bermuda, Canada, Colombia, the Dominican Republic, El Salvador, Guam, Guatemala, Indonesia, Japan, the Republic of Nauru, the Netherlands, New Zea-

land, Nicaragua, Panama, Singapore, Sweden, the United States, Venezuela and the host Taipei.

Porter said that the Philippines, Zimbabwe and New Guinea previously had said they would send teams. Porter said if their entries came in within the next few days, the ISF would consider them.

By The Associated Press

this time had become the centerpoint of a political struggle between two nations located halfway around the world from his home base in Oklahoma.

Public sentiment was so strong that Porter was notified only a couple of days into the event that the government of Taiwan had received a number of threats on his life. He was provided with an around-the-clock secret service detail that shadowed him for the remainder of the event. "I remember deciding to go downstairs to pick up a newspaper in the lobby of my hotel. The minute I stepped into the hallway, four armed secret service agents immediately joined me and cleared my path."

The measures were necessary due to the fact that protesters had begun to assemble outside the hotel. "There must have been a couple hundred people outside. A couple of the signs caught my attention. They read 'Kill Porter.'"

Porter was advised to leave the country immediately upon completion of the event for his own safety, foregoing the typical summary work normally involved in an event of this magnitude. To make matters worse, the USA team finished fourth, the only medal-less performance in the USA's history. "This was without a doubt the hardest six months of my life to that point," he said. Unfortunately for Porter, there were more difficult personal moments ahead of him.

In time, Porter was able to remove himself from the political issues that had haunted him and refocus on his job of campaigning for softball's addition to the Olympics. By 1985, Porter was beginning to feel confident that softball was inching closer to its goal. Samaranch continued to counsel Porter to remain patient. Porter was convinced that with the addition of such sports as team handball, table tennis, badminton and tennis to the program, softball's position in the pecking order was near the top.

Samaranch suggested that perhaps the best way to move softball along was to form an alliance with baseball. Porter took the suggestion and flew to Lausanne, Switzerland to discuss the particulars with Bob Smith of baseball. Porter attended the 1985 IOC Congress in Lausanne with high expectations that this would be the end of the campaign. Sports are added to the program seven years out, so softball's focus was on a debut at the 1992 Olympics Games in Barcelona. What had seemed like softball's inevitable moment of triumph ended in frustration when support for the softball/baseball pairing broke apart, led by a number of Latin American representatives who favored men's baseball over women's softball. Baseball was in. Softball was out. "I was happy for Bob Smith and baseball, but devasted for softball," Porter said.

Later attempts to get softball on the program in Barcelona as an exhibition sport along with golf also dissolved as the IOC executive committee turned down a recommendation by the Barcelona Organizing Committee, citing organizational problems with the 1992 Games.

Softball

DON E. PORTER
Executive Director

20 September 1988

TO: ASA Council Members

FROM: Don Porter, Executive Director

RE: Olympic Status for Softball

As most of you are aware the Olympic Games are presently going on in Seoul. In addition, the International Olympic Committee (IOC) held its General Session just prior to the start of the Games.

Your president (Bert Weeks), immediate past president (Andy Loechner) and I, attended the IOC meetings to represent softball's interest in becoming a new medal sport on the Olympic Program.

As many know and those who don't....we have been actively involved during the past ten years to bring about Olympic status for softball. This has not been an easy course and has been most frustrating, mainly from the stand-point of having to contend with the way the IOC conducts its business.

We have been assured on several occasions by the IOC and its president, that softball would in time, be included as a medal sport on the Olympic Program.

We have most recently worked closely with baseball, mainly at the encouragement of the IOC, in proposing baseball (men) and softball (women) as the best route to gain Olympic status. This was pursued, however, in 1986, the IOC, in its infinite wisdom, approved baseball and not softball. However, the IOC agreed to reconsider softball and it was placed back on the agenda for the next IOC Session in Calgary (February 1988), a week prior to the Calgary IOC Session, we were informed the decision on softball was postponed until the IOC Session at Seoul (September 1988).

During the IOC Session in Seoul this past week, the softball question did come before the Session. A number of IOC members rose during the discussion in support of softball. However, IOC President Samaranch advised the program for Barcelona (1992) had been closed and no further sports could be added to the program. Since there was strong support for softball by a number of IOC members it was agreed that it would be taken up at the next IOC Session in Puerto Rico, August 1989. A decision on the 1996 program will be taken at that time.

AMATEUR SOFTBALL ASSOCIATION OF AMERICA

NATIONAL ASA HEADQUARTERS and HALL OF FAME • 2801 N.E. 50th St. • Oklahoma City, Oklahoma 73111 • (405) 424-5266

It was the opinion of the IOC that adding the pressure of two more sports, exhibition or otherwise, would add too much stress on an already struggling local organizing committee.

The disappointment was so intense that Porter for the first time considered throwing in the towel. "I came home devastated and talked with my people. I asked them straight on. Do you want to continue or is this it?" Porter said. After the pain of the initial blow had subsided, the only answer was to press on.

And, press on he did. Porter next found himself at the 1988 Olympic Games in Seoul, Korea, this time as Chairman of the Transportation Committee for the United States Olympic Committee

(USOC). Porter's position gave him continued access to the decision makers in the Olympic movement. Little did he know that perhaps the greatest challenge to his quest was directly ahead. One day in Seoul, Porter was making his rounds at the hotel when he inadvertently turned a corner smacking into an IOC member from Ireland. Embarrassed, Porter apologized before continuing on. In the collision, Porter had injured his foot and was in constant pain throughout the rest of the week. After visiting a sport's trainer at the event, he was advised that the injury appeared to be a deep bruise,

ASA Council
20 September 1988
Page two

In the meantime, the only door left open for 1992 is the possibility of softball being an exhibition sport in Barcelona. We have submitted an application for women's softball and hope to hear something around the end of October.

While this has been most frustrating to many of us, we were encouraged by the wide support from IOC members during the Session in Seoul and President Samaranch's words during my meeting with him at Seoul; "you must be patient, it took baseball 25 years to get in." Our response to President Samaranch; "while we have not been at it 25 years, it seems like it!"

While the delay on softball's acceptance is disappointing, it is certainly not the end of the game, we must go on to strengthen and improve our domestic programs and organization and help when and where we can to continue the development of the sport both domestically and internationally.

Our big disappointment is for the athletes who are deprived of the Olympic experience and the recognition a sport receives in attaining Olympic status. On behalf of President Weeks, Andy Loechner, Bill Kethan and many others, we appreciate the support and the understanding from many of you who believe that softball should have Olympic status.

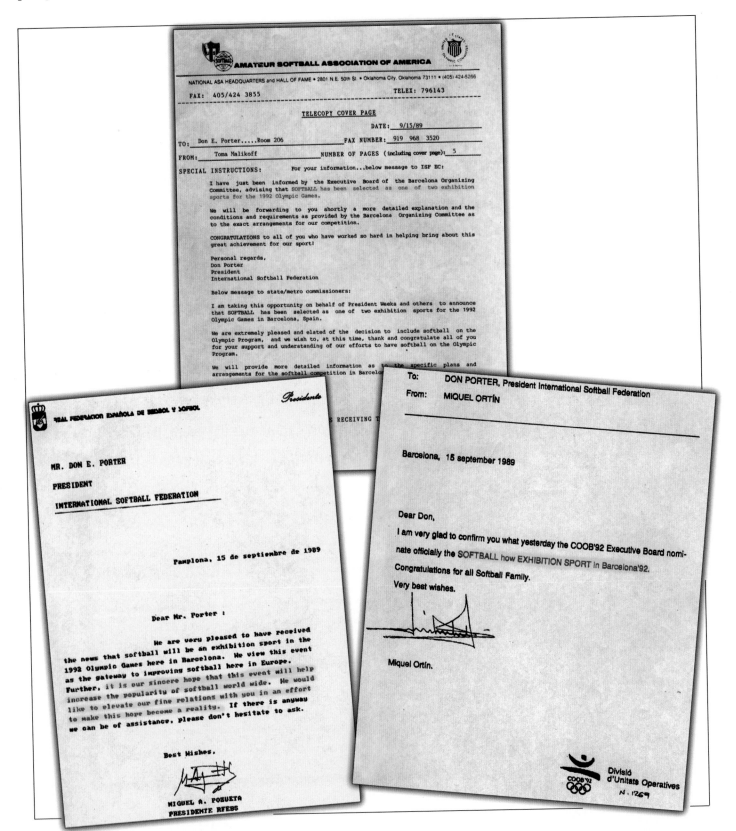

AMATEUR SOFTBALL ASSOCIATION OF AMERICA

NATIONAL ASA HEADQUARTERS and HALL OF FAME • 2801 N.E. 50th St. • Oklahoma City, Oklahoma 73111 • (405) 424-5266

FAX: 405/424 3855   TELEX: 796143

TELECOPY COVER PAGE

DATE: 9/15/89

TO: Don E. Porter.....Room 206   FAX NUMBER: 919 968 3520

FROM: Toma Malikoff   NUMBER OF PAGES (including cover page): 5

SPECIAL INSTRUCTIONS: For your information...below message to ISF EC:

I have just been informed by the Executive Board of the Barcelona Organizing Committee, advising that SOFTBALL has been selected as one of two exhibition sports for the 1992 Olympic Games.

We will be forwarding to you shortly a more detailed explanation and the conditions and requirements as provided by the Barcelona Organizing Committee as to the exact arrangements for our competition.

CONGRATULATIONS to all of you who have worked so hard in helping bring about this great achievement for our sport!

Personal regards,
Don Porter
President
International Softball Federation

Below message to state/metro commissioners:

I am taking this opportunity on behalf of President Weeks and others to announce that SOFTBALL has been selected as one of two exhibition sports for the 1992 Olympic Games in Barcelona, Spain.

We are extremely pleased and elated of the decision to include softball on the Olympic Program, and we wish to, at this time, thank and congratulate all of you for your support and understanding of our efforts to have softball on the Olympic Program.

We will provide more detailed information as to the specific plans and arrangements for the softball competition in Barcelona.

REAL FEDERACION ESPAÑOLA DE BEISBOL Y SOFBOL   *Presidente*

MR. DON E. PORTER

PRESIDENT

INTERNATIONAL SOFTBALL FEDERATION

Pamplona, 15 de septiembre de 1989

Dear Mr. Porter :

We are very pleased to have received the news that softball will be an exhibition sport in the 1992 Olympic Games here in Barcelona. We view this event as the gateway to improving softball here in Europe. Further, it is our sincere hope that this event will help increase the popularity of softball world wide. We would like to elevate our fine relations with you in an effort to make this hope become a reality. If there is anyway we can be of assistance, please don't hesitate to ask.

Best Wishes,

MIGUEL A. POZUETA
PRESIDENTE RFEBS

To: DON PORTER, President International Softball Federation

From: MIQUEL ORTÍN

Barcelona, 15 september 1989

Dear Don,

I am very glad to confirm you what yesterday the COOB'92 Executive Board nominate officially the SOFTBALL how EXHIBITION SPORT in Barcelona'92.

Congratulations for all Softball Family.

Very best wishes.

Miquel Ortín.

Divisió
d'Unitats Operatives
COOB'92
N. 1769

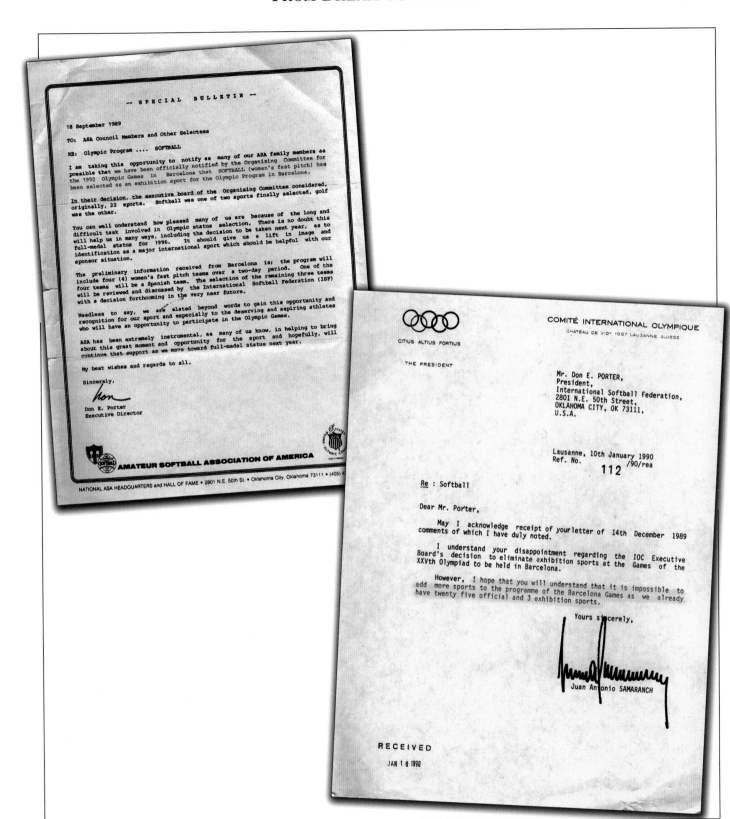

-- SPECIAL BULLETIN --

18 September 1989

TO: ASA Council Members and Other Selectees

RE: Olympic Program .... SOFTBALL

I am taking this opportunity to notify as many of our ASA family members as possible that we have been officially notified by the Organizing Committee for the 1992 Olympic Games in Barcelona that SOFTBALL (women's fast pitch) has been selected as an exhibition sport for the Olympic Program in Barcelona.

In their decision, the executive board of the Organizing Committee considered, originally, 22 sports. Softball was one of two sports finally selected, golf was the other.

You can well understand how pleased many of us are because of the long and difficult task involved in Olympic status selection. There is no doubt this will help us in many ways, including the decision to be taken next year, as to full-medal status for 1996. It should give us a lift in image and identification as a major international sport which should be helpful with our sponsor situation.

The preliminary information received from Barcelona is; the program will include four (4) women's fast pitch teams over a two-day period. One of the four teams will be a Spanish team. The selection of the remaining three teams will be reviewed and discussed by the International Softball Federation (ISF) with a decision forthcoming in the very near future.

Needless to say, we are elated beyond words to gain this opportunity and recognition for our sport and especially to the deserving and aspiring athletes who will have an opportunity to participate in the Olympic Games.

ASA has been extremely instrumental, as many of us know, in helping to bring about this great moment and opportunity for the sport and hopefully, will continue that support as we move toward full-medal status next year.

My best wishes and regards to all.

Sincerely,

Don E. Porter
Executive Director

AMATEUR SOFTBALL ASSOCIATION OF AMERICA

NATIONAL ASA HEADQUARTERS and HALL OF FAME • 2801 N.E. 50th St. • Oklahoma City, Oklahoma 73111 • (405) 4

CITIUS · ALTIUS · FORTIUS

THE PRESIDENT

COMITÉ INTERNATIONAL OLYMPIQUE

CHATEAU DE VIDY 1007 LAUSANNE SUISSE

Mr. Don E. PORTER,
President,
International Softball Federation,
2801 N.E. 50th Street,
OKLAHOMA CITY, OK 73111,
U.S.A.

Lausanne, 10th January 1990
Ref. No. 112 /90/rea

Re : Softball

Dear Mr. Porter,

May I acknowledge receipt of your letter of 14th December 1989 comments of which I have duly noted.

I understand your disappointment regarding the IOC Executive Board's decision to eliminate exhibition sports at the Games of the XXVth Olympiad to be held in Barcelona.

However, I hope that you will understand that it is impossible to add more sports to the programme of the Barcelona Games as we already have twenty five official and 3 exhibition sports.

Yours sincerely,

Juan Antonio SAMARANCH

RECEIVED

JAN 1 6 1990

but that he should have it checked upon his return home.

The injury did not improve and Porter scheduled a visit with his doctor in Oklahoma City. The trainer's diagnosis turned out to be correct. However, on further examination of Porter, a lump was found on his neck. "How long has that been here," the doctor asked. Porter replied "for awhile, but it comes and goes."

After further testing, Porter was advised to remove the lump. Testing confirmed the worst. The tumor was malignant and Porter's next challenge would be against lymphoma cancer. Over the course of the next eight months, Porter underwent chemotherapy, losing his hair and substantial weight. "The treatments destroyed my appetite and energy," he said.

Porter missed few days at work during the treatments. "When I got tired, I would rest for an hour and then resume. The focus on my work helped keep the focus off my problem," he said.

Amazingly Porter took few respites during the period and continued to fly around the world, still driven by his mission to make his Olympic dream a reality. One trip included a meeting with Samaranch in Portland, Oregon. "Samaranch and I had become friends over the years and he asked me with genuine concern how I was doing? I told him that I was making the most of it and that my work and goals had not changed."

Porter's cancer was diagnosed as level one and offered a 70 percent reversal rate. His doctors suggested that the stress associated with his Olympic quest may in fact have contributed to his ailment. "I guess I'll never know the cause. I do believe, however, it was my family and my work that kept me alive during this difficult time," he said.

By 1991, Porter was beginning to see signs of a breakthrough as more and more IOC officials began to verbalize their support for the sport. Porter traveled to the 1991 IOC session in Birmingham, England with then current and former ASA presidents Bill Smith and Andy Loechner. The IOC meetings were closed to non-voting members, but Porter remembers numerous

ABOVE: *ASA President Bill Smith, Don Porter and former ASA President Andy Loechner in Barcelona for 1991 Olympic Announcement.*

Photo courtesy of International Softball Federation

COMITÉ INTERNATIONAL OLYMPIQUE
CHÂTEAU DE VIDY. 1007 LAUSANNE. SUISSE
CASE POSTALE 356, 1001 LAUSANNE
☎ 25 32 71/72/73 ⓣ 454 024 CH · FAX 021 24 15 52 ⚑ CIO Lausanne
BANQUE: UNION DE BANQUES SUISSES. CH. POST. 10-2282

CITIUS · ALTIUS · FORTIUS

Mr. Don E. PORTER
President
Fédération Internationale de Softball
P.O. Box 11437
2801 N.E. 50th Street
OKLAHOMA CITY / Oklahoma 73111
United States

Birmingham, 16th June 1991
Ref. no.   2851   /91/jsb

Re : Games of the XXVI Olympiad, Atlanta 1996

Dear Mr. Porter,

Following the meeting of the 97th IOC Session here in Birmingham, I have pleasure in informing you that it has been decided, in agreement with the Atlanta Committee for the Olympic Games, to add women's softball to the programme of the Games of the XXVI Olympiad, Atlanta 1996.

The softball tournament will comprise 8 teams.

This decision has been taken on an exceptional basis, for the Games of the XXVI Olympiad only, due to softball's popularity in the United States. Final arrangements for the tournament are to be discussed between the IOC, your Federation and the Atlanta Committee for the Olympic Games. I am of course at your disposal for any further information in this respect.

Yours sincerely,

Gilbert FELLI
Sports Director

individuals giving him positive reports on the progress of the meeting. Porter, however, refused to get his hopes up this time. "As far as I'm concerned it's not official until it's official."

Finally, Samaranch exited the meeting and spotted Porter standing overlooking the rails of the balcony above the meeting site. Samaranch stopped in front of Porter and offered the words he had waited to hear for a lifetime. "Finally, Mr. President, finally." The IOC session adjourned with a press conference and softball's addition to the program of the 1996 Olympic Games was confirmed. Softball was now an Olympic sport.

Porter had realized his Olympic dream and was destined to throw out the first

Atlanta
1996

August 12, 1991

Mr. Don E. Porter
President
International Softball Federation
2801 N.E. 50th Street
Oklahoma City, Oklahoma 73111

Dear Don:

I sincerely apologize for not responding sooner to your kind letter of thanks for our support in gaining the approval of the inclusion of women's softball in the program for the Olympic Games in Atlanta in 1996. Needless to say, we are excited to have women's softball on the program and are looking forward to working with you to make the competition here in Atlanta an exciting and memorable one.

I must tell you that any of our efforts on behalf of women's softball pale into insignificance when compared to your steadfast and unswerving commitment to including women's softball in the Olympic program. We have all watched with great admiration your tireless devotion to this cause and especially your courage in the face of adversity.

All of us in Atlanta greatly appreciate your support of our efforts but most of all we value greatly your friendship. We are looking forward to working with you and your colleagues in the International Softball Federation to organize an outstanding competition in Atlanta.

I remain

Sincerely yours,

William Porter Payne
President and
Chief Executive Officer

RECEIVED
AUG 1 5 1991

ce for the Olympic Games
, GA 30301 - 1996 USA   Phone 404-224-1996   Fax 404-224-1997

Don Porter announces that women's fast-pitch softball will be considered a medal sport at the 1996 Olympics in Atlanta.

Softball's Gold Rush On for '96

By Murray Evans
Staff Writer

As a young, eager campaigner for Olympic recognition of softball in 1968, Don Porter received some advice from then-International Olympic Committee president Avery Brundage: Be patient, and your sport's time will come.

It took 23 years, but softball has finally joined the Olympic family of sports. At its annual session last Friday in Birmingham, England, the IOC voted to add women's fast-pitch softball as a medal sport for the 1996 Games in Atlanta.

"We're very pleased that softball finally has made the grade," said Porter, executive director of the Oklahoma City-based Amateur Softball Association and president of the International Softball Federation, during a press conference Monday at the ASA Softball Hall of Fame. "This is something many of us here and around the world who have supported softball have been waiting a long time for."

The IOC vote came after a recent major disappointment in softball's quest for recognition at the Olympic level. Women's fast-pitch had

See SOFTBALL, Page 23

pitch, happy to have been a part of the process and finally cancer-free.

ABOVE: *Jean Porter, Juan Antonio Samaranch, Don Porter and Andy Loechner at Olympic Games.*
Photo courtesy of International Softball Federation/Bob Moreland.

OPPOSITE PAGE (CLOCKWISE FROM TOP LEFT): *Porter at Superball '95 in Columbus, Ga.;*
Porter offers congratulations to USA Softball National Team Member Trish Popowski; Porter and Olympian Leah O'Brien;
and Porter thanking fans and community at Superball '95. Photos courtesy of USA Softball/Doug Hoke.

3

THE
LEGACY
OF
WINNING

LEFT: *The USA Team past and present.*
Foreground photo courtesy of USA Softball/Doug Hoke.
Background photos courtesy of National Softball Hall of Fame.

Few sports programs, professional or amateur, can match the achievements of USA Softball women's national teams over the last three decades. In World Championship and Pan American Games competition dating back to 1965, the USA has amassed a lifetime record of 125-12 (97 wins by shutout), outscored their opponents 806-85, and brought home the gold nine times and the silver four others.

Since 1986, the USA has totally dominated the sport winning three consecutive World (1986, 1990, 1994) and Pan American Games gold medals (1987, 1991, 1995).

Amazingly their current winning streak in World and Pan Am play is 63-0.

Since softball's birth in Chicago, Illinois in 1887, the United States has been a leader in the development of the sport worldwide but they have not been the only country lobbying for its growth and recognition. In fact, the concept behind the sport's first World Championship was actually initiated by the Australian Women's Softball Council under the direction of president Esther Deason. In 1962, Australia council members Deason, Merle Short and Marjorie Dwyer attended the World Softball Series held in Stratford, Connecticut, which featured 19 teams, including entries from the United States, Japan and Canada.

The Australian officials believed that it was time for the sport to have its own international softball series to determine a world champion. With the support of Amateur Softball Association and International Softball Federation president W.W. "Bill" Kethan and ISF Secretary/Treasurer Don Porter the concept was approved and Australia was sanctioned as the site for the first ISF Women's World Championship in 1965. The tournament boasted an outstanding international field of five teams: the host team Australia, New Zealand, Japan, New Guinea and the United States.

. . . .
LEFT: *Sydney Opera House, Sydney, Australia.*

OPPOSITE PAGE (BACKGROUND): *1990 World Team.* Photo courtesy of USA Softball/Ron Babb

The USA, represented in Melbourne by the Raybestos Brakettes of Stratford, Connecticut, the reigning Amateur Softball Association women's major national champion, came into the tournament heavily favored despite the fact that the event was played in February, months after the Brakettes' season had ended.

The Australians put a damper on the U.S. team's plans by seizing the moment early in the round robin and inflicting a 3-1 first round loss to the USA. The USA responded with consecutive wins over New Zealand, 1-0; and New Guinea, 7-0, 8-0 and then redeemed themselves with a 1-0, 10-inning defeat of the host team. However, the battle for the title was just beginning.

The USA added wins over New Zealand and Japan to improve to 5-1 and claim a semi-final rematch with the Aussies. No one could have predicted the outcome.

Australia paired solid hitting and magnificient fielding against USA errors and completely outplayed the Americans to win the contest 7-0 before a stunned audience. Australia out-hit the USA 7-3, but perhaps the biggest factor in the loss was the USA's defensive lapses which accounted for four errors and the lopsided score. Even the USA's legendary pitching ace, Bertha Tickey, could not slow the onslaught and left the game due to injury.

But the USA had not come halfway around the world to get their reputations and posteriors kicked from the team from down under. They took their frustration out on Japan 6-0 behind the pitching of 18-year old Donna Lopiano who had replaced Tickey, 41, due to her previous injury. The combination of Lopiano's two-hit performance and Kathryn "Sis" King's power hitting, that included two triples and three RBI, blasted the USA into a title game rematch with Australia.

For five innings, the USA's Lopiano and Australia's Lorriane Woolley battled to a scoreless tie. The USA appeared on the threshold of breaking the game open in the third when the leadoff hitter singled and was bunted to second. With two outs, the runner advanced to third on an error, but the threat evaporated when the Australian left fielder "Houdini'd" a diving catch to end the inning.

The damage came in the sixth when Australian Eleanor McKenzie led off with a double to center. One batter later, USA pitcher Lopiano uncorked a wild pitch that rocketed over catcher Laura Malesh's head scoring McKenzie who never broke stride as she turned from third and made a diving head-first slide into home just ahead of Malesh's tag.

Three up and three down in the top of the seventh for the USA and the first world championship was in the record books...with Australia bringing home the gold.

I'll have to use that one.

OPPOSITE PAGE (TOP): *Bertha Tickey.*

OPPOSITE PAGE(BOTTOM): *Donna Lopiano.*

RIGHT: *1965 World Champion Team, Australia.*
Photos on these pages courtesy of National Softball Hall of Fame.

Although the USA displayed some veiled great moments, it was not the dominating start that many had predicted. But it was a beginning; the American's had embarked on their quest to become the best in the world.

These softball pioneers will always be remembered for their contributions to the sport. They were what no one else can ever be: the first.

Included among the membership of the USA's first world team were some of the sport's legends including future Hall of Fame members Bertha Tickey Ragan (1972), Donna Lopiano (1983), Pat Harrison (1976), Kathryn "Sis" King (1975) and Rosemary "Mickey" Stratton (1969). Also on the team were Anna De Luca, Millie Dubord, Edna Fraser, Beverly Danaher, Mary Bennett, Laura Malesh, Brenda Reilly and Carol La Rose. Amateur Softball Association Hall of Honor members William S. Simpson was general manager and Vincent "Wee" Devitt team manager.

LEFT: *Play at Home statue at the National Softball Hall of Fame.*

OPPOSITE PAGE: *1965, from left, Bertha Tickey, Wee Devitt and Kathryn (Sis) King. In front are Carol LaRose and Mickey Stratton. King, Tickey and Stratton are members of the National Softball Hall of Fame. Devitt is a member of the Hall of Honor. Photos on these pages courtesy of National Softball Hall of Fame.*

The ISF World Championships moved to Osaka, Japan in 1970 with the field of teams increasing to nine including defending champion Australia, Canada, China, host Japan, Mexico, New Zealand, the Philippines, the United States and Zambia.

In this competition, the USA was represented by the Orange Lionettes, the 1969 ASA Women's National Champions, and led by player/manager Carol Spanks, player/coach Shirley Topley and coach Rosalie Sorenson.

The USA won their first two contests impressively beating Zambia 13-2 in six innings and New Zealand 4-0. However, history was about to repeat itself.

The USA's third contest against the Philippines was scoreless into the seventh inning when Philippines leftfielder Carmelita Apolinario delivered a single off Nancy Welborn in the bottom of the seventh scoring teammate Leticia Gempisao who had earlier beat out an infield hit to short.

When Apolinario singled to right, Gempisao broke for home and was at first called out at the plate after catcher Nancy Ito took a throw from USA rightfielder Mickey Davis in time to make the tag. Ito dropped the ball during the collision at the plate. The run counted and the upset was in the books.

The USA regrouped and posted four consecutive wins over Mexico, 10-0; Australia, 1-0; Canada, 2-1; and China, 5-0. They added a fifth win in a row by tarnishing Japan's perfect record 1-0 to knot the USA's and Japan's round robin records at 7-1.

In the semi-finals, Japan beat defending champion Australia 4-0 and the USA avenged its earlier defeat by beating the Philippines 1-0. The Philippines then beat Australia 1-0 for the bronze medal, setting up a final game showdown for the gold between Japan and the USA.

The final drew more than 30,000 spectators to the Nagai Stadium in Osaka. Much to the delight of the huge crowd, Japan managed to overcome an outstanding two-hit pitching performance by Nancy Welborn and score the winning run in the third inning on a bizarre series of events. Japan's Seiko Katsumata opened the inning with a walk and was sacrificed to second on a bunt. After a strikeout of the next batter, the USA had two outs and it appeared they would escape the inning untarnished until Junko Matsuda bunted and instead of a routine out, Welborn overthrew teammate Topley at first. Second baseman Rose Adams retrieved the ball and launched it to the plate, but Matsuda beat the throw to score what turned out to be the winning run.

It is ironic that in two world championship finals, the USA pitching staff – known as the best in the world – lost both contests on errant throws.

Team Win, Team Loss!

OPPOSITE PAGE: *1970 World Team represented by Orange Lionettes*

LEFT: *Nancy Welborn. Photos on these pages courtesy of National Softball Hall of Fame.*

Two world championship silver medals and an overall record of 16-5 was not a bad start by most measures, but one that the USA was determined to improve upon in the years ahead.

The ISF World Championship made its first visit to American soil in 1974 in Stratford, Connecticut, and the USA began its trek to softball supremacy behind the artistry of legendary pitcher Joan Joyce and the coaching of Ralph Raymond, who would lead the USA to multiple world titles in the years to come.

Something was definitely different about the 1974 USA team. In the previous championships, the USA had challenged, but they had not dominated. In just four years, the USA was able to separate itself from the rest of the field in impressive fashion — posting nine consecutive shutouts and outscoring their opponents 75-0 in the process.

USA pitchers Joan Joyce and Pat Whitman produced a perfect team ERA of 0.00 which included 90 strikeouts in 56 innings. Joyce was especially impressive posting 76 of the strikeouts and allowing only three hits in 36 innings.

The USA also dominated at bat collectively producing 84 hits for a team batting average of .356. Six players batted above .300 including Irene Shea (.500, 14 hits, 12 runs, three RBI, four stolen bases); Willie Roze (.455, 10 hits, seven runs, seven RBI, five stolen bases); Kathy Elliott (.444, 12 hits, 13 runs, 11

WORLDS 1974

LEFT: *Ralph Raymond.* Photo courtesy of National Softball Hall of Fame.

RBI; Joan Joyce (10 hits, four runs, 10 RBI); Joan Moser (eight hits, eight runs, 6 RBI); and Joyce Compton (seven hits, nine runs, seven RBI).

Eleven new world records were established at the 1974 event including five by Joyce. Joyce set records for most strikeouts (76); lowest ERA (0.00); consecutive scoreless innings (36); most no-hit, no-run games (3); and most perfect games (2).

The USA's performance was the most dominating of any team in softball history and the first indication that something truly special was on the horizon for the Americans.

The tournament itself was also beginning to show signs of significant growth with a field of 15 teams in three divisions now competing for the world title. Over 100,000 spectators attended the 9-day event including 12,500 for the title game.

The USA found itself facing some old challengers in the 1974 event including Japan and Australia, who completed the championship with the silver and bronze. However, the USA's combination of power pitching, hitting and sparkling defense, the standard of Raymond managed teams of the future, worked on everyone, including Japan and Australia. The USA outscored Australia and Japan collectively for the event 18-0, surrendering only one hit between them in the process.

The title game was scoreless after three innings until the USA's Kathy Elliott looped a fly ball down the right field line

LEFT: *Peggy Kellers.*
Photo courtesy of National Softball Hall of Fame.

for a double and was sacrificed to third by team-mate Joyce Compton. Japan made a tactical error by walking the USA's next two batters, Joan Joyce and Cec Ponce, to face Willie Roze who took advantage by doubling to right to score Elliott and Joyce. Ponce also reached the plate on a wild pitch by Japan starter Mikoyko Naruse.

Japan's offensive plan was to bunt their way to the title. Every Japanese batter tried to bunt in the first four innings with the exception of Naruse, who besides getting the start in the title game also lead Japan in the tournament as a hitter. Japan's plan was not

productive as it created only one hit against the USA's Joyce.

Following the USA's big fourth inning which left them three runs behind, Japan began to hit away but Joyce fanned eight of the last nine batters to finish with 15 strikeouts for the game.

The USA had turned the corner and won their first world championship in convincing fashion. It was a precursor of things to come. The dynasty that would soon become synonymous with USA Softball had begun to come of age.

· · · · · · · · · ·

ABOVE: *1974 World Team represented by the Brakettes.*

OPPOSITE PAGE: *Joan Joyce.*
Photos on these pages courtesy of National Softball Hall of Fame.

The USA's domination continued at the 1978 World Championships in San Salvador, El Salvador, but with a new set of challengers that included a controversial entry: the Chinese Taipei team.

For the first time in women's softball's history, the spectre of politics entered the scene. The International Softball Federation (ISF) had awarded the 1978 World Championship to Canada in 1975. However, when the Canadian government learned that Taiwan (Chinese Taipei) might be numbered among the participants, they quickly notified the Canadian Softball Association there would be no Canadian government financial support.

The ISF then awarded the game to Japan following its 1977 ISF Congress in Johannesburg, South Africa, but the Japanese were also forced to withdraw on April 10, 1978 due to political pressure. Businessmen in the Nagoya industrial area where the event was scheduled feared economic reprisals from China, which resulted in their withdrawal of financial support for the championship. Japan tried to have the event shifted to a secondary site in the north suburbs of Tokyo, but the facilities were deemed inadequate and not up to ISF World Championship standards. The scene next shifted to Tokyo itself, but China succeeded in stopping the process again.

ISF Secretary-General Don Porter commented that the "World Championship being held in Japan was probably not an earth shaking development in light of other world problems, but what is important is the fact that the ugly face of politics in sport had risen again."

ISF President W.W. "Bill" Kethan, using his best diplomacy, commended Japan for their leadership and for their attempts to make the championship work, but also said he was "disappointed that the government of Japan had allowed the People's Republic of China to intimidate them."

In other political matters, Mexico and the Philippines were suspended by the ISF in 1976 after withdrawing from the Men's World Championship in New Zealand in protest of the entry of South Africa. The withdrawal was interpreted as a violation of ISF rules which prohibit "political interference by any government into the internal operation or function of a national sports governing body." The suspension prohibited the Philippines and Mexico from participating in any international competition including the Women's World Championship in 1978.

The South African Softball Association was already under investigation by the ISF due to complaints of racial discrimination in their policies. Amidst the turmoil of their own social problems, South Africa was suspended by the ISF during the investigation, but reinstated in 1977 following satisfactory resolution of the problems. Despite their reinstatement, South Africa did not reappear in international competition until 1996 at the ISF Men's World Championship in Midland, Michigan.

The tournament, politically marred and missing strong contenders in Japan and the Philippines, went on as scheduled. Despite the problems, fifteen nations including Canada, Australia, the Netherlands, El Salvador, Puerto Rico, Guatemala, Zambia, New Zealand, Chinese Taipei, Bahamas, Italy, Belize, Panama and Nicaragua competed for the title.

The USA, represented again by the Brakettes, emerged from the tournament unde-

feated on the strength of its newest pitching stars Kathy Arendsen and Barbara Reinalda. Arendsen tied Joan Joyce's record for the lowest ERA (0.00, 33 innings) and most no hitters (3). Reinalda pitched a three-hitter in the title game to defeat Canada 4-0. Arendsen and Reinalda combined for 11 consecutive shutouts in the event.

The U.S. collectively outscored their opponents 61-0 and posted an impressive .325 team batting average. The team featured strong offensive performances, including Joan Van Ness (.407, 11 hits, seven runs, five RBI, three triples); Kathy Strahan (.400, 14 hits, 12 runs, 4 RBI); Susan Enquist (.379, 11 hits, seven runs, seven RBI); Marilyn Rau (.346, nine hits, four runs, 10 RBI); and Diane Schumacher (.343, 12 hits, nine runs, five RBI and a triple).

The first team to win two consecutive World Championships, the USA took a 19-0 winning streak with them into the 1982 competition in Taiwan.

BACKGROUND: *Kathy Arendsen*
Photo courtesy of National Softball Hall of Fame.

W
O
R
L
D
S

1
9
8
2

The 1982 World Championships saw a new representative for the USA in the Orlando Rebels, the 1981 ASA Women's National Champions coached by Marge Ricker.

The lineup was absent some of the USA's recent heroes, but featured another consortium of talented performers including shortstop Dot Richardson and pitcher Debbie Doom.

The USA extended their international winning streak through the round robin with shutouts of Australia, 4-0; Singapore, 4-0; Columbia, 10-0; Guatemala, 10-0; Belgium, 8-0; and Sweden, 9-0. The winning streak increased to 25-0, all by shutout, and the USA appeared on their way to winning their third consecutive World Championship.

However, following the round robin, USA team members made their only venture into local cuisine and spent the remaining days of the tournament shuffling between the field and the public restrooms with widespread dysentery. USA shortstop Dot Richardson remembers all too well the situation. "I remember being in the women's restroom between innings and hearing my name announced over the loud speaker as the next batter. It was an experience I wouldn't want to relive."

The USA dropped their next game 2-1 to host Chinese Taipei before winning their next contest against the Philippines 5-0. The USA lost another game to Chinese Taipei, 1-0 and was then eliminated by Australia 1-0.

The USA placed fourth, the only medal-less performance in the program's history. "We received a fourth place medal made of iron. I still remember standing on the medal stand before 30,000 roaring Chinese Taipei fans wearing my iron medal. I'm sure it was an emotional thing, but that medal was the heaviest thing I have ever had around my neck. I swore that it would never happen again," Richardson said. New Zealand went on to win the 1982 championship with a 2-1 win over Chinese Taipei who took the silver. Australia took home the bronze.

The USA, represented again by the Brakettes, started a new winning streak at the 1986 World Championship in Auckland, New Zealand winning 13 straight games to reclaim the gold medal they had lost in 1982.

The USA pitching staff of Kathy Arendsen (4-0), Barbara Reinalda (4-0), Lisa Ishikawa (3-0) and 16-year-old Michele Granger (2-0) recorded an incredible 172 strikeouts and allowed only one earned run (Reinalda) during the competition.

The USA offense outscored their opponents 38-4 led by Dot Richardson (.318), who made her second consecutive world championship appearance after making the move to the Brakettes from the Orlando Rebels.

Against China in the final, MVP Kathy Arendsen was spotted a two-run lead in the fourth by teammate Jackie Gaw who drilled a two-out single to center. That was all the cushion Arendsen needed as she closed out the contest and the win at 2-0 for the gold medal.

WORLDS 1986

LEFT: *MVP Kathy Arendsen.*

OPPOSITE PAGE: *1990 World Team.*
Photos on these pages courtesy of National Softball Hall of Fame.

The World Championship returned to the United States in 1990 and the USA team took full advantage hammering out 10 consecutive wins to take the rain soaked tournament in convincing style.

Entering the medal rounds the USA remained the only undefeated team at 9-0, followed by New Zealand, China and Australia at 8-1. New Zealand's only loss came in their sixth game against Chinese Taipei.

In a semi-final showdown, Suzy Brazney and Xan Silva drove in two runs each to lead the USA to a lopsided 6-1 win over New Zealand. New Zealand forced a rematch with the USA in the final by beating China 1-0.

Torrential rains delayed much of the play in the final days of the tournament and interrupted the gold medal game after three scoreless innings. Over the protest of New Zealand coach Ed Dolejs, the gold medal was eventually awarded to the USA according to ISF rules by virtue of the USA's perfect record in pool play. Dolejs contended that New Zealand should be named co-champion despite their earlier 6-1

WORLDS 1990

The 1990 USA Team featured no shortage of pitching talent with Becky Duffin, Lisa Longaker, Lisa Fernandez, Kathy Arendsen and Debbie Doom combining for 96 strikeouts in nine games (10.6 average) with eight shutouts, four no-hitters and a perfect game by Longaker.

The USA also featured a powerful offensive attack that outscored their opponents 79-2. Batting leaders included Mary Lou Flippen (.667, 10 hits, nine runs, one triple, three doubles, six RBI); Sheila Cornell (.556, 15 hits, 11 runs, one homer run, seven doubles, eight RBI); Pam Newton (.500, 14 hits, 10 runs, one triple, one double, five RBI); and Dot Richardson (.500, five hits, four runs, two triples, three RBI).

The USA introduced several newcomers to its lineup, but none more spectacular in her debut than Lisa Fernandez who produced shutout wins against Puerto Rico and Japan, went 3-for-3 at bat and was perfect in the field in eight attempts.

loss to the USA. USA head coach Raymond argued that the Americans had not been beaten, even though New Zealand had the chance, and should be named champion.

The ISF agreed and the USA was on its way to establishing its latest international win streak that included another two consecutive world titles and a 23-0 record against its opponents. Head coach Ralph Raymond improved his record to 32-0 and three World Championship titles in as many attempts.

The USA Softball Women's National Team captured their third consecutive ISF World Championship in the 1994 ISF Women's World Fast Pitch Championship at the Caribou Memorial Complex in St. John's, Newfoundland, Canada.

The USA breezed through the round robin section of the tournament with an unblemished record of 6-0, then won four more games in the eight-team playoffs to emerge with its fifth ISF World Championship since 1965 and third in a row (1986, 1990 and 1994). In the Grand Final, before a crowd of more than 7,500 people, the USA blanked China, 6-0, collecting 10 hits off three Chinese pitchers.

However, China gave the USA one of its best games of the tournament in game 10 of the playoffs, before losing 2-1 in 12 innings. The USA, which had then won 32 games in a row in ISF World Championship play, tied the score in the bottom of the sixth and pushed the winning run across in the 12th on a throwing error made by the Chinese third baseman.

The USA's offensive leaders included Julie Smith, who contributed 11 hits, 10 RBI, two home runs and a batting average of .344. Smith provided several game-winning hits during the tournament including one each in the USA's first and second playoff wins over Australia (1-0, 2-0). Smith's most dramatic moment, however, came in the title game against China when she broke the game open with a two-run blast in the fifth inning.

WORLDS 1994

RIGHT: *Julie Smith had a home run up her sleeve in the final at the 1994 Worlds.*
Photo courtesy of USA Softball/Ron Babb
OPPOSITE PAGE: *Signposts at 1990 Worlds.*
Photo courtesy of International Softball Hall of Fame.

The USA's offensive weapons were many including leading hitter Dot Richardson, who produced 13 hits, nine runs and three RBI. Other leaders included Lisa Fernandez (.393, 11 hits, six runs); Sheila Cornell (.357, 10 hits, seven runs); and Smith (.344, 10 hits, 11 runs).

In the final, China asserted its challenge early against USA pitcher Lori Harrigan managing runners at first and second with one out in the top of the first. China appeared on the threshold of producing the game's first score when Fang Yan drove a pitch to deep center. The USA's Laura Berg responded with a perfect one-hop strike from center to teammate Karen Sanchelli who made the tag at the plate. Harrigan fanned the next Chinese batter and the threat was over.

Harrigan was admittedly nervous early but settled down and did not allow a runner past second the rest of the way. The USA, meanwhile delivered a hitting clinic of their own beginning with two runs in the fifth inning and four more in the sixth.

Julie Smith drew first blood with a two-run blast in the fifth with no outs that scored teammate Dot Richardson who was already aboard.

The strength of the USA was reflected in the cumulative stats that included a team batting average of .317 and a pitching staff (Michele Granger, Susie Parra, Lori Harrigan, Michele Smith and Lisa Fernandez) that allowed only two earned runs in 65 innings, while striking out 100 batters. The five allowed only 18 hits and finished with a team ERA of 0.22. On defense, the USA made only three errors for a .988 fielding percentage.

· ·

OPPOSITE PAGE (TOP): *Thumbs up: Michelle Gromachi, Michele Smith, Barbara Jordan and Dot Richardson. Photo courtesy of USA Softball/Ron Babb.*

OPPOSITE PAGE (BOTTOM): *Lisa Fernandez with 1994 World Championship Medal. Photo courtesy of USA Softball.*

BACKGROUND: *Pledging their allegiance are Michele Smith and Julie Smith. Photo courtesy of USA Softball/Ron Babb.*

ABOVE: *1994 World Team cheering at the award ceremony.* Photo courtesy of USA Softball/Ron Babb.

LEFT: *Martha O'Kelley and USA are number 1.* Photo courtesy of USA Softball/Ron Babb.

OPPOSITE PAGE: *1994 World Championship Team at Oklahoma Capitol.* Photo courtesy of USA Softball.

The USA's great success in the World Championships was mirrored in the Pan Am Games. Following an exhibition performance in 1967, softball was officially added to the program in 1979. The USA took the gold in 1979 in San Juan, Puerto Rico with a 13-1 record, winning 13 games by shutout and outscoring the competition collectively 74-2. The team was led by an outstanding pitching performance by Kathy Arendsen (0.00 ERA), Barbara Reinalda, Paula Noel and Melanie Kyler. Marilyn Rau led the tournament in hitting with an outstanding .464 batting average. USA coaches Ralph Raymond and Lorene Ramsey also made their Pan American Games debut.

The USA began the competition with three consecutive shutouts against Canada (1-0), El Salvador (10-0) and the Dominican Republic (5-0) before falling to the tiny nation of Belize, 2-1, in game four. Belize, despite their lack of exposure to world class competition, continued as one of the event's giant killers and eventually won the bronze.

The USA did not remain off track for long and strung together eight consecutive wins to finish the round robin at 11-1. It was payback time in the playoffs with the USA blasting Belize, 6-0, to earn the gold medal game against host Puerto Rico, which they won 2-0.

. . . .

BELOW: *Reinalda/Kethan at medal ceremony of 1979 Pan American Games.*

OPPOSITE PAGE: *1979 Pan American Team.*
Photos on these pages courtesy of National Softball Hall of Fame.

Despite a better overall record and two previous lopsided wins against Canada (6-0, 7-1), the USA lost the one that counted in the 1983 Pan Am final to Canada, 5-4. This was the first and only silver medal for the USA in Pan Am play.

The USA stumbled out of the gate, losing their first game of the competition to Puerto Rico 6-5. But the deficit was quickly overcome as the USA responded with nine consecutive wins to finish the round robin with the best record at 9-1.

In the first game of the playoffs, the USA handed Canada an impressive 7-1 defeat that included a two-hit pitching performance by American ace Kathy Arendsen.

USA pitcher Lori Stoll, who had delivered two no-hitters and a four-hitter in her earlier Pan Am start, got the call against Canada in the final. Canada scored two in the second, one in the third and two more in the fourth to take a commanding 5-1 lead into the sixth inning.

The USA bats rallied in the sixth when Pat Dufficy and Diane Schumacher produced consecutive doubles. Teammate Deanne Moore followed with a triple to score Dufficy and Schumacher to cut the score to 5-3. The USA appeared on the verge of completing a dramatic come from behind victory when Sheila Cornell singled to score Moore and bring the Americans within a point of matching the Canadians. Unfortunately, the USA's bats went silent and Canada closed out the win to take the championship and finish 9-3, despite the USA's better record of 10-2.

The USA completed the competition outscoring their opponents 104-23 and recording six of their wins by shutout. The 1983 championship was clearly one that the USA let slip away.

. . . .

OPPOSITE PAGE: *Dianne Schumacher.*
Photo courtesy of Dianne Schumacher.

From 1987 - 1995, the USA was in control of the Pan Ams, stringing together 9-0, 9-0 and 12-0 performances in Indianapolis, Indiana; Santiago de Cuba and Parana, Argentina.

In Indianapolis, the USA team featured veterans Dot Richardson and Sue Gaw along with Pan Am newcomers in Michele Granger, Rhonda Wheatley and Ella Vilche, who combined to produce eight shutouts in nine games during the competition. The USA outscored the competition collectively 51-1, including three wins over runner-up Puerto Rico 4-0, 4-0, 4-1. Richardson provided the offensive spark scoring 10 runs and hitting three triples, including one that put the game out of reach of Puerto Rico in the final.

By the third inning of the final against Puerto Rico, the USA had a 4-0 lead. Pitcher Ella Vilche gave up the USA's only run of the competition in the final when Janice Parks of Puerto Rico hit a triple and then scored on a sacrifice by teammate Jackeline Ortiz.

. . . .

LEFT:
Coach Ralph Raymond.

BELOW:
The late Alison Rioux in action.

OPPOSITE PAGE:
Newcomer Michele Granger.
Photos on these pages courtesy of National Softball Hall of Fame.

THIS PAGE: *Celebrating the Gold in 1987.*

OPPOSITE PAGE: *Waving the flag.* *Photos on these pages courtesy of USA Softball.*

The USA continued their dominance in 1991 in Santiago de Cuba behind the smothering pitching performances of Lisa Fernandez, Debbie Doom and Michele Granger and a lethal offensive attack that outscored their opponents 60-3.

The gold medal game was for all purposes over in the first inning. The USA scored 11 runs in the bottom of the first, enroute to an easy 14-1, five-inning rout of Canada, completing a 9-0 sweep of the competition.

The USA sent 15 batters to the plate in the first inning of the final and began the pounding when Denise Day knocked in the first run on a ground out. With the score 3-0, designated hitter Camille Spitaleri stepped to the plate and smashed a two-run single. Second baseman Julie Smith followed with a two-run single up the middle. First baseman Sheila Cornell followed with a two-run double and Day drove in the 11th run of the inning with a single.

The USA scored again in the third on an RBI single that scored Julie Standering. Standering provided two RBI of her own in the fourth on a single that pushed the score to 14-1. USA pitcher Lisa Fernandez recorded her fifth consecutive win of the competition.

USA pitchers dominated the Games, allowing 13 hits, three runs and fanning 110 in 60

innings including a pair of perfect games thrown by Debbie Doom who went 3-0. Doom was later named the Wide World of Sports' Player of the Week for her efforts. Granger finished at 1-0, sidelined early due to a cut on her pitching hand.

Eight players batted above .300 including Trish Johnson (.500, six hits); Mindy Jenkins (.462, six hits); Denise Day (.429, nine hits); Camille Spitaleri (.400, six hits); Debbie Hoddevik (.364, four hits); Kris Schmidt (.357, five hits); Suzy Brazney (.350, seven hits) and Sheila Cornell (.312, six hits).

. . . .

ABOVE: *1991 Pan American Team.*

OPPOSITE PAGE: *Wide World of Sports' Player of the Week, Debbie Doom.*
Photos on these pages courtesy of National Softball Hall of Fame.

In 1995, the event moved to Parana, Argentina, and the USA produced what may be its most dominating performance to date in the competition.

The USA finished the round robin portion of the 1995 event 10-0 with impressive wins over Puerto Rico, 6-0; the Netherland Antilles, 11-0; Canada, 6-1; Cuba, 1-0; Argentina, 11-0; Puerto Rico, 14-0; Netherland Antilles, 10-0; Canada, 2-0; Cuba, 2-0; and Argentina, 11-0.

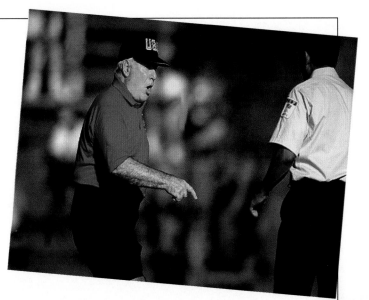

In the semifinals, the USA faced a tough opponent in Cuba who had already given the Americans two of their toughest tests of the competition. Lefthander Michele Granger of the USA responded pitching a perfect game (5-0) that included 16 strikeouts on 100 pitches.

The USA scored twice in the first when Dot Richardson and Julie Smith singled and advanced a base on a sacrifice by teammate Pat Dufficy. Richardson scored on an illegal pitch by Cuban starter Estela Milanes. Sheila Cornell followed with a single that scored Smith.

Cornell opened the fourth inning

with a triple and scored moments later when Michele Smith delivered an inside-the-park home run, her third in the competition.

In the gold medal game, Michele Smith produced a one-hit, 4-0, shutout against Puerto Rico, finishing the competition at 3-0. The win pushed the USA's international win streak in World and Pan Am play since 1986 to 63-0 and 104-0 in major international competition during the same period. Smith, who struck out nine batters, limited Puerto Rico to a single hit in the

PAN AM GAMES 1995

ABOVE RIGHT: *Coach Raymond makes a point.*

LEFT: *Michele Smith.*

OPPOSITE PAGE: *1995 Pan American Team.*

Photos on these pages © 1995 Tielemans Photography

second inning and never allowed a runner past second. She also drove in the USA's first run in the second inning with a single that scored Kim Maher, who had singled and advanced to second on a wild pitch.

The USA added insurance runs in the sixth on RBI singles by Maher and Cornell. It was the second Pan American Games gold medal for head coach Ralph Raymond (1979, 1995).

The USA's pitching staff was near perfect with Debbie Doom (2-0), Michele Granger (4-0), Lori Harrigan (2-0) and Susie Parra (2-0) producing a combined ERA of 0.00. Michele Smith (3-0) gave up the lone run of the event, an inside-the-park home run against Canada to finish with an ERA of 0.37. Collectively, the pitching staff put up some incredible numbers including 11 shutouts, 146 strikeouts and a team ERA of 0.09.

Granger paced the team with four wins, including a perfect game to eliminate Cuba in the semi-finals. She also led the team in strikeouts with 57 in 24 innings and gave up only three hits in the competition. Smith was close behind with three wins and 33 strikeouts in 19 innings.

The USA offense was also impressive producing a team batting average of .380 led by Cornell at .581 with 18 hits, nine runs, three triples, three doubles and eight RBI. Michele Smith demonstrated her versatility by not only producing three wins from the circle, but leading the team in home runs with three and batting .429 with 12 hits, five runs and 14 RBI, including four game winners.

Ten USA batters hit over .300 including Cornell (.591); Karen Sanchelli (.500); Jill Justin (.500); Ann Rowan (.500); Dot Richardson (.469); Martha O'Kelley (.438); Michele Smith (.429); Kim Maher (.375); Patty Benedict (.333); and Shelly Stokes (.308).

In World Championship and Pan American Games competition, the USA has been unreachable, particularly in the last decade. Since their international debut at the World and Pan Am's, the USA has won an amazing nine gold and three silver medals in 13 attempts. The winning legacy that has become USA Softball is also far from over as the sport approaches the new millennium and the 2000 Olympic Games.

RIGHT: *Sheila Cornell and Fans.*

BELOW: *Congrats.*

OPPOSITE PAGE: *Dot's swat.*

Photos on these pages © 1995 Tielemans Photography

MANY ARE CALLED, FEW ARE CHOSEN

The June 13, 1991 announcement in Birmingham, England that the International Olympic Committee had included softball on the program of the 1996 Olympic Games in Atlanta, Georgia sent shock waves through the softball community.

The softball community, although eternally optimistic on the surface, had become cautious and at times even guardedly cynical about the prospects, particularly the players. After all, the sport had been proposed as a demonstration sport, an exhibition sport and even promised a spot in Barcelona in 1992, all to be told later that it would not happen.

But this announcement was different. Amateur Softball Association of America (ASA) officials Don Porter, executive director, then-president O.W. Bill Smith of Nebraska, and former-president Andy Loechner, Jr. of Pennsylvania were front and center in Birmingham to hear the formal announcement. Finally, the decision was real and a part of public record. Softball was in the Olympics.

The announcement sent tremors not only through the softball community at-large but the ASA as well. The ASA had campaigned the hardest of any for the honor and now it was time for them to make the most of the opportunity. It was not enough for softball to be on the program, their charge would be to first earn membership among the eight teams that would compete and then to not only win, but win big in the Olympics.

It was a charge that officials at the ASA took very seriously.

The search for America's finest women softball players was officially on.

The process of selecting USA National Teams in the past had been a simple one. When the USA needed a representative at an international competition such as the World Championships they sent the USA's reigning national champions. For the Pan American Games, the association conducted a weekend tryout camp with the top 18 selected for the competition.

The procedure was not perfect, but it had produced multiple World and Pan American Games champions. However, it had also produced runner-up finishes at the 1965 and 1970 World Championships and for the only time in the history of the program a medal-less performance at the 1978 World Championships.

By most measurements USA Softball's medal production during the program's history

. . . .

OPPOSITE: *Flags at Golden Park*
Photo courtesy of International Softball Federation/Bob Moreland
ABOVE: *Golden Park, home of the Columbus Red Stix, was soon to undergo extensive renovation before its emergence as the site of the 1996 U.S. Olympic Softball competition.*
Photo courtesy of USA Softball/Doug Hoke

USA SOFTBALL NATIONAL TEAM SELECTION COMMITTEE

One of the most difficult and no-win, no-thanks jobs leading up the Olympics was that of membership on the National Team Selection Committee.

With thousands of athletes in competition for 15 positions, the task of sorting through the talent and making the final selections was grueling and involved hundreds of hours of critique and evaluation of players coast to coast.

The committee membership included a wide circle of softball representation from such groups as the ASA, the NCAA, Special Olympics International, the National Junior College Athletic Association (NJCAA) and former elite softball athletes.

Their job was specific, but not easy. Select the nation's best fifteen softball athletes to represent the USA in softball's first Olympics. This committee of unheralded volunteers would never receive the accolades deserving of their contribution to the process, but they would draw great satisfaction that when all was complete they had produced a team that would bring home USA gold in 1996.

PAT LILLIAN

Pat Lillian, chairperson from Anchorage, Alaska, represented the ASA. Her background includes extensive experience in softball administration as the Alaska ASA commissioner. She has received numerous sports related service awards including the Alaska First Lady Volunteer Award and the Alaska 49er Sports Award.

(continued next page)

All National Selection Committee members photos provided by USA Softball

was exceptional. However, ASA officials understood fully the expectations of softball's ardent group of followers and that anything less than gold in the sport's first Olympics would be viewed, fairly or not, as a disaster for the program.

The Olympics was different than any other event in the program's history and in the eyes of the ASA and America's recognition-hungry softball family its crown jewel, the gold medal, of supreme importance. The Olympics symbolized the best in athletics and the ASA was doggedly determined to put the finest 15 players from the land on the field in 1996.

This began an extensive rethink of the whole process for selecting USA Softball National Teams. The concept shifted from a team concept to an individual all-star selection process that would ultimately include thousands of Olympic hopefuls from every point in the land.

The doors thrown wide open, how would the ASA control the onslaught of prospects that would likely emerge and how would the field be ultimately reduced to the final 15 who would compete?

It was a monumental challenge that the ASA tackled with bravado. First on the list was the establishment of a national coaching pool and a national team selection committee.

ASA officials believed that in the process of providing the best players in the land, they must insure that those players would be mentored by the finest coaches in softball.

Pivotal to the success of the program was the establishment of the USA Softball National Team Selection Committee. This committee was charged with the difficult and sometimes unpopular task of making the final cuts on teams that would represent the USA at every international competition leading up to the Games and ultimately in deciding who would be on the final Olympic team as well.

The final selection committee consisted of chair Pat Lillian, Ronnie Isham, Kathy Arendsen, Star Orullian, Jay Miller, Karen Sykes and Irene Shea. Over the course of the next three years, the lives of these individuals changed dramatically as they collectively logged hundreds of thousands of miles of travel in order that they might watch, examine, evaluate and critique

IRENE SHEA

Irene Shea, representing the NCAA, participated on numerous ASA national championship teams and was a member of the 1974 USA World Championship team. Shea was also a three-time ASA All-American with the Raybestos Brakettes and a former NCAA softball coach.

JAY MILLER

Jay Miller, representing Special Olympics International, is head softball coach at the University of Missouri and a member of the ASA Foreign Relations Committee. He has conducted numerous softball workshops nationally and internationally and has conducted coaching and player clinics in Holland, France, Czechoslovakia and Italy.

KAREN SYKES

Karen Sykes, representing the NJCAA, has been a high school and college softball coach for over two decades. She served on the Pan American Games Selection Committee in 1987 and 1991 and is a member of the ASA Foreign Relations Committee.

(continued next page)

RONNIE ISHAM

Ronnie Isham, representing the ASA, has been involved in softball for over 25 years as a player, manager and an ASA Player Representative from Texas. Among his duties was team leader for the USA Softball Junior Men's Team that competed in the World Championship in Auckland, New Zealand in 1993.

KATHY ARENDSEN

Kathy Arendsen was one of two elite athlete representatives on the committee. During her 15-year career with the Raybestos Brakettes, Arendsen played on nine ASA national championship teams and is a 13-time ASA All-American. She has extensive playing experience and represented the USA in the 1978, 1986 and 1990 World Championships and the 1979 and 1983 Pan American Games.

STAR ORULLIAN

Star Orullian was the second elite athlete representative on the committee. Orullian is a veteran of international competition including the 1983 Pan American Games and the Nichi Cup in Japan. She is also a three-time ASA All-American and the ASA Commissioner for Utah.

players anywhere elite softball was being played.

One of the committee's first priorities was the selection of a national coaching staff. The list included eight of the nation's most experienced, accomplished and revered softball coaches including Ralph Raymond, head coach of the famed Raybestos Brakettes and a multiple gold medal winner as coach of USA National Teams in World and Pan Am competition; Mike Candrea, head softball coach at the University of Arizona; Sue Enquist, co-head softball coach at UCLA; Ralph Weekly, head softball coach at the University of Tennessee-Chattanooga; Margie Wright, head softball coach at Fresno State University; Diane Schumacher, head softball coach at Augustana College and Carol Spanks and Shirley Topley, both members of the National Softball Hall of Fame and seasoned USA National Team coaches.

· ·

OPPOSITE PAGE(TOP LEFT): *National Team Coach Diane Schumacher conducting hitting practice.* Photo © 1995 Arlan Flax/Alfa Photography

OPPOSITE PAGE(TOP RIGHT): *USA Softball National Team Coach Shirley Topley putting the players through warm-ups.* Photo © 1995 Arlan Flax/Alfa Photography

OPPOSITE PAGE(BOTTOM): *Shelly Stokes, Coach Topley, Coach Raymond and Coach Ralph Weekly.* Photo ©1995 Tielemans Photography

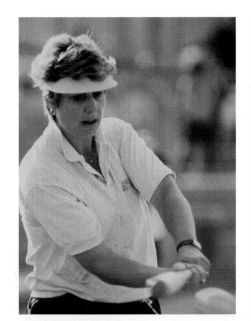

NATIONAL TEAM COACHES

One of the first responsibilities of the National Team Selection Committee was to select the coaches who would lead USA Softball national teams in various competitions during the quadrennium leading up to the sport's Olympic debut in 1996. Among the competitions were the 1994 Pan American Games Qualifier in Guatemala, the 1995 Jr. Girl's World Championship, the 1995 Pan American Games, Superball '95 and finally the Olympic Games.

Just as the players knew that ultimately only fifteen would advance to the Olympic Games, the National Team coaches also knew only three would get the call in 1996.

RALPH RAYMOND

Among the eight coaches was Ralph Raymond, head coach of the Raybestos Brakettes of Stratford, Connecticut. In Stratford, he produced 18 ASA National Champions and finished as runners-up seven times.

In international play, he coached USA teams to gold medals in four World Championships and three Pan American Games competitions.

MIKE CANDREA

Mike Candrea, head coach of the Arizona Wildcats, was also among the eight. Among Candrea's accomplishments were NCAA National Championship titles in 1991, 1993, 1994 and 1996. Under his leadership, Arizona has reached the

NCAA Women's College World Series nine consecutive years.

SHIRLEY TOPLEY

Shirley Topley has had a distinguished career as both a player and coach as noted by her election to the National Softball Hall of Fame in 1981. As a player she was a member of six ASA National Championship teams. She has helped coach the USA to five

gold medals including the 1990 World Championships and the 1991 and 1995 Pan American Games.

SUE ENQUIST

Sue Enquist also demonstrated great success as a player and coach, winning a gold medal at softball's debut in the 1979 Pan American Games. As a coach she helped lead the USA to a 15-0 pounding of the competition in the 1994 Pan American Games Qualifier in Guatemala. She is the head softball coach at UCLA and helped lead the Bruins to national titles in 1992 and 1995.

CAROL SPANKS

Carol Spanks was inducted into the National Softball Hall of Fame in 1981 in tribute to her success as a player that included membership on four ASA National Championship teams, 13 All-American selections and 19 national championship appearances. Internationally, Spanks played in the 1970 ISF World Championships in Osaka, Japan and helped coach the USA to gold medals at the 1985 and 1994 South Pacific Classic and the 1987 Pan American Games.

RALPH WEEKLY

Ralph Weekly is among the nation's most successful collegiate coaches with NAIA national titles in 1988 and 1992. He was named NAIA National Coach of the Year eight times.

Internationally, Weekly has helped lead the USA team to a gold medal at the 1994 Pan American Games Qualifier, Superball '95 and the 1995 Pan American Games.

MARGIE WRIGHT

Margie Wright is among the nation's winningest collegiate coaches, with her Fresno State teams advancing to the NCAA regionals each year during her tenure and to the

Women's College World Series in seven of the last ten years. As a player, Wright is a four-time ASA All-American. She has helped lead USA teams to gold medals at the 1991 Pan American Games and the 1995 Jr. Girls' World Championship.

DIANE SCHUMACHER

As a player Diane Schumacher won gold medals for the USA at the 1979 Pan American Games and the 1978 World Championships. She is a seven-time ASA All-American and a member of the National Softball Hall of Fame and the ISF Hall of Fame. She continues as the head softball and basketball coach for Augustana College in Rock Island, Illinois.

The committee selected its first all-star national team in 1992 for the Challenger Cup in Beijing and again in 1993 for the Intercontinental Cup in Holland. The contests measured the USA team against the best teams in Asia and Europe and the program against itself. The results were even better than anyone had hoped as the USA pounded out impressive and dominating wins in both events.

At the Challenger Cup, the USA women, led by pitchers Lisa Fernandez, Susie Parra, Lori Harrigan, Debbie Doom and Michele Smith went 8-0 with a perfect team ERA of 0.00 and outscored their opponents 29-1. The following year they repeated the pattern in Holland at the Intercontinental Cup with a 9-0 run that included defeats of Canada, China, Australia and Chinese Taipei, all of whom would soon be faced at the 1994 World Championships and ultimately the Olympic Games.

The USA had its first solid evidence that the process was following the correct path for gold in Atlanta.

All National Team Coaches' photos courtesy of USA Softball with the exception of Diane Schumacher's, which appears courtesy of Diane Schumacher.

From the announcement in 1991 until the Olympics in 1996, softball seemed to enter its own time warp with everything that happened on the elite level somehow becoming uncharacteristically important. Almost everything that happened to USA Softball since the June 13 decision was a first-ever undertaking and historically significant in context, at least within the confines of amateur sport.

With the national coaches and selection committee in place, the hard work of creating a blueprint to steer the program to the gold was finalized. Almost two years in development and spearheaded by selection committee chair Pat Lillian, a plan was developed, refined, refined again and finally implemented. The course set, USA Softball was on its way to Atlanta.

In 1993, the U.S. Olympic Festival became a major tool in the development of USA Softball's elite athlete pool. It marked the first time that USA Softball had used the event as a pivotal component of its player identification, selection and development program.

Previous Festivals included the top four women's and men's teams from the ASA major nationals but did not address the qualifications of individual players on the team. If a team finished in the top four, the whole team received the "perk" of playing in the Festival.

For the first time, players would have to earn their spot based solely on their own personal merit. Making a Festival became absolute proof that you were among the top 60 players in the nation at that time.

USA Softball also imple-

RIGHT: *The competition for the Olympic team begins among the elite at the 1993 Festival.*
Photo ©1993 Ben Van Hook/DUOMO Photography

RIGHT: *Running for the gold.*
Photo © 1993 Ben Van Hook/DUOMO Photography

OPPOSITE PAGE: *Olympic hopeful taking her cuts.*
Photo © 1994 Arlan Flax/Alfa Photography

mented a national team tryout program in 1993 that included its first USA Softball Women's National Team Camp. One hundred and seven of the sport's top identified women's fast pitch players participated in a week-long event at USA Softball's official training facility in Oklahoma City. An invitation to this camp was a confirmation of a player's ability and a major step to the realization of the Olympic Dream.

In 1994, the blueprint called for a national tryout process that resulted in the creation of the largest elite player database in the sport's history. The plan was designed to provide players from every destination in the country a shot at making this historic team and to discover the unsung heroes, if any, that had somehow been overlooked.

The potential numbers were staggering. An estimated 50,000 players were expected to compete for 15 positions on the Olympic team. It was to say the least an organizational challenge, but although ambitious, it was certainly in line with the serious attitude that USA Softball had taken concerning the selection of this first Olympic team.

Players were screened at the starting level for elite softball skills. If those elite skills were indeed verifiable, the athlete received an invitation to a USA Softball Level I tryout camp

There are some at Bloom

geographically located at 10 points across the nation in 1994 including Sacramento, California; Arlington, Texas; Marietta, Georgia; Springfield, Massachusetts; Lawrence, Kansas; Long Beach, California; Dekalb, Illinois; Columbus, Ohio; Tempe, Arizona; and East Lansing, Michigan.

One of the early invitations went to a 16-year-old at Dobie High School in Houston, Texas. "When I received an invitation to the Level I tryouts it was a surprise because I didn't know I had applied," said Christa Williams. Turns out that her dad, Ed Williams, did not want to potentially disappoint Christa so he sent in the application for her.

"I remember reporting to the Level I tryouts in Texas. They brought out this board with a hole cut out in the strike zone. I remember thinking to myself, 'I'll never be able to hit that.'

"It was pretty stressful. There was this radar gun pointed at me and people standing around

taking notes. I still wonder what they were writing," Christa said.

Stressful undoubtedly for Christa and thousands of others, but necessary to trim the large field down to the elite group that would be invited to attend the USA Level II Camp.

Christa made the grade and advanced not only to the Level II Camp but on to Level III. She ultimately received an invitation to the USA Softball Women's National Team Camp in September 1994 in Oklahoma City. Christa, virtually unknown at the national level when the process began, went on to earn a spot on the 1994 USA Softball Women's Pan Am Qualifier Team, the 1995

Junior Girls' National Team and eventually the 1996 Olympic Team.

Christa was proof positive that the process was working and a new generation of softball heroes was being discovered along the way.

By 1994, the process was in full swing and prestigious spots on USA Softball National Teams were on the line. Among those opportunities was the 1994 ISF World Championship July 24-August 7 in St. John's, Newfoundland, Canada. Seventeen were selected following the 1994 U.S. Olympic Festival in St. Louis, Missouri to defend the USA's two prior consecutive world titles. As the Olympics drew closer, each competition grew in significance.

Very Good Lead!

Julie Smith stood motionless, eyes closed, seemingly overwhelmed by what was happening to and around her. Could it be true? Had the USA actually won their third consecutive world title and had her home run actually been the difference? A myriad of thoughts raced through her mind, including a flashback to her mammoth swat and her triumphant trek to home.

Alongside, the beaming faces of teammates Michele Smith and Lisa Fernandez told another story as they hoisted a traditional "number one" salute to the crowd —a gesture that appeared more of a "we actually did it" statement than one of self-recognition.

Further down the line, veteran Dot Richardson, blocking out the mayhem of her surroundings, focused intently on each note of the national anthem as it resonated through the public address system at the stadium. A tear cascaded down her cheek.

ABOVE: *They're number one! Michelle Gromacki, Lisa Fernandez, Michele Smith, Barbara Jordan, Dot Richardson, Jenny Condon and Laura Berg at the 1994 World Championships.*
Photo courtesy of USA Softball/Ron Babb

OPPOSITE PAGE: *Christa Williams pitching at the 1995 Jr. Worlds.*
Photo © 1995 Todd Rosenberg/All Sport USA, appears courtesy of USA Softball

It was a euphoric and incredibly emotional moment. In perhaps their greatest test leading up to the 1996 Olympic Games, the ladies of USA Softball had proven they were undisputedly the best in the world.

"These players know how to win. When the game is on the line there is no talk about next time. They're number one in the world because they know how to reach down and come up with some- thing extra. No one does that better than our players," said head coach Ralph Raymond.

Raymond himself knows something about winning, having coached 18 national champions with the famed Raybestos Brakettes of Stratford, Con- necticut. His record five World Championship gold medals as coach of the USA Softball Women's National Team is unchallenged.

Despite the USA's propensity for the gold and the fact that the World Champi- onship was the major qualifying event for the sport's first Olympics, the event went virtually unnoticed by the national media who seemed enamored with the prospects of a threatened baseball strike.

Although the attention of the world seemed directed elsewhere, the ladies of USA Softball went about their duties of winning ball games and the hearts of thousands who filled the grandstands in St. John's.

Bloom SB

For Julie Smith it was a tournament she will never forget. Smith delivered key hits throughout, particularly when the field narrowed and the medals were on the line. In playoff competition, Smith was responsible for the game-winning RBI in all but one game, her biggest in the fifth inning of the gold medal game when she launched a two-run boomer over the centerfield fence. The blood drawn, the USA went on a 10-hit, six-run frenzy to bury a very capable opponent in China.

"Someone on our team was going to step up and get the key hits. This time it happened to be me, but it could have been anyone on the team, I'm that confident of my teammates," Smith said.

The World Championship decided five of the eight teams that would compete in Atlanta in 1996, including China, Canada, Australia and Chinese Taipei. The USA was already guaranteed a slot before the tournament because of their position as host country.

When asked if the victory in the World Championships meant as much to the USA since their place in the Games had already been secured, Smith replied that the "USA doesn't play for berths, it plays to win. When I wear the letters USA across my chest, I'm playing for my country. There is nothing more important to me than that. This win was very important to all of us."

RIGHT: *1994 World Champions Sheila Cornell, Gillian Boxx, Martha O'Kelley, Susie Parra and Michele Granger. Photo courtesy of USA Softball.*

OPPOSITE PAGE: *Coach Raymond. Photo courtesy of USA Softball.*

Michele Smith of Califon, New Jersey and Lisa Fernandez of Long Beach, California, two of the sport's most consistent performers, were not at the top of their game during the week. Smith, who had burned a stellar international field with three home runs just a month prior at the South Pacific Classic in Sydney, batted a slight .167 at the Worlds. Fernandez, who had paced the USA to a gold medal at the 1991 Pan American Games, posted an uncharacteristic 2.00 ERA in her only start.

The USA's victory was the model of good team play. When the stars struggled, their less heralded — but equally talented — teammates stepped up to take command.

"Rookie" Laura Berg of Santa Fe Springs, California made her international debut batting .385 and producing some of the competition's most exciting moments in the outfield, including her perfect bullet to home from center field to pick off a Chinese runner at the plate in the title game.

Sheila Cornell of Diamond Bar, California, a 32-year-old three-time Pan American Games and World Championship gold medalist made her contribution batting .357 with 10 hits and scoring the game-winning run in a must-win semi-final performance against China.

Pitchers Susie Parra of Scottsdale, Arizona; Lori Harrigan of Las Vegas, Nevada; and Michele Granger of Anchorage, Alaska each contributed two important wins and posted a combined ERA of 0.00.

Martha O'Kelley of Huntington Beach, California; Jenny Condon of Edina, Minnesota; Karen Sanchelli of Columbia, South Carolina; Barbara Jordan of Huntington Beach, California; Pat Dufficy of Stratford, Connecticut; Jill Justin of Oaklawn, Illinois; Gillian Boxx of Torrance, California; and Michelle Gromacki of Antioch, California all helped make a difference on the field. Corporately they contributed a team batting average of .317, including 70 runs on 83 hits against four runs for their opponents. As a team defensively, they were nearly perfect with only three errors in 65 innings.

I wish we could do this!

Despite Fernandez's struggles from the circle, she made big contributions at third with a flawless defensive effort and at the plate with 11 hits and a batting average of .393.

Michele Smith, silent at the bat in the early going, delivered her hits when the medals were on the line and went 2-0 from the mound, including a gutsy 12 inning 2-1 marathon win over China in the playoffs to earn the USA their place in the gold medal game.

Dot Richardson of Orlando, Florida understood the significance of the moment as well as perhaps anyone. Her professional and personal sacrifices behind her for the moment, she would soon return to her medical duties at the University of Southern California Medical center as a four-time World Champion.

"People sometimes have no idea what kind of personal sacrifice is required to stay competitive at this level. I've had a dream of playing in the Olympics since I was a child. As much as I love my medical career, I'll put it on hold for a year if necessary to make that team," she said.

At the World Championships, Richardson delivered 13 hits, including two doubles, in 33 at-bats for an average of .394. Her fielding percentage at short was perfect (1.000).

In St. John's, the top guns of every nation in the world lined up to take their shots at the legend that had become USA Softball. The ladies of USA Softball responded with proof positive that they are the best in the world.

There were a number of other important competitions along the way that helped form the equation that would produce the final team selections for the Olympic Games, including the 1994 Pan Am Qualifier in Guatemala, the 1995 Pan American Games in Parana, Argentina, the 1995 Junior Girls' World Championship in Normal, Illinois, the 1995 U.S. Olympic Festival and Superball '95 in Columbus, Georgia.

BACKGROUND: *The 1994 USA World team after their selection at the U.S. Olympic Festival in St. Louis, MO.*
Photo courtesy of USA Softball.

Despite the USA's position as reigning Pan American Games champions they were required to compete in the 1994 Pan Am Qualifier in Guatemala. Fighting mosquitoes, no hot water and other third world conditions, the USA demonstrated once more that they were serious about their march to the sport's first Olympics in 1996, winning 15-0 and outscoring their opponents 119-0.The team featured six eventual Olympians including Lisa Fernandez, Christa Williams, Leah O'Brien, Gillian Boxx, Dionna Harris and Dani Tyler as well as alternates Michelle Venturella, Jennifer McFalls and Dee Dee Weiman.

It was the international debut for Christa Williams. If she was nervous about her debut it didn't show. In her first outing against El Salvador, she pitched a no-hitter and followed four games later with a one-hitter against Belize. Williams' 15-0 perfect game performance against Nicaragua launched her into the national and international spotlight. Williams ended her Guatemala debut with a 0.00 ERA, three shutouts and 45 strikeouts.

In March of 1995, the USA Softball women took their third consecutive gold medal at the Pan American Games. When the USA Softball Women's National Team headed into the Pan American Games in Argentina they had a lot more than a medal riding on the outcome.

First, they had an incredible winning streak to protect as well as a shot at the history books as the first women's team to win three consecutive gold medals.

A ballgame or two into the competition and it was already apparent. There was the USA and then there was the rest of the field. The battle was not for gold, that was already settled, but for second and third positions on the medal stand.

Twelve consecutive wins and the USA women were once again champions and their international win streak reached an incredible 104-0. In an Associated Press story by Barry Wilner he commented that the streak was "the longest of any sport on record and likely a record that would probably never be broken."

Statistically, the USA women were unreachable, giving up one run against 83 of their own. The competition never had a chance as the USA scattered 114 hits including 14 doubles, 15 triples and three home runs. The USA shooters were deadly posting a team ERA of 0.09 with 11 shutouts, five one-hitters, two two-hitters and perfect games by Debbie Doom and Michele Granger.

The USA Softball winning machine was moving toward Atlanta and picking up momentum at every turn.

. . . .

TOP RIGHT: *Lori Harrigan.*

BOTTOM RIGHT: *Ann Rowan and fans.*

OPPOSITE PAGE: *Michele Granger pitching.*

Four months later, America's future was under examination at the Junior Girls' World Championships in Normal, Illinois. True to their winning heritage, the USA Softball Junior Girls' World Team dominated the competition with a 15-0 performance. This sent out a message to the world that the USA planned to continue dominating the sport not just in 1996, but in the 2000 Games and beyond.

Christa Williams' ability was already apparent, but her mental grit was never better demonstrated than in a gutsy performance against China. Facing her first batter in the game, Williams was called for an illegal pitch. Turning to get a better look at the umpire's call, Williams momentarily looked away just as her catcher released the ball back to

. . . .

ABOVE: *Play at home at 1995 Jr. Worlds.*

LEFT: *Christa Williams airborne in celebration after winning the gold medal at the Junior Worlds.*

OPPOSITE PAGE (BOTTOM LEFT): *Christa Williams pitching.*

OPPOSITE PAGE (BOTTOM RIGHT): *Don Porter presenting medal.*

OPPOSITE PAGE (BACKGROUND): *The USA Softball Junior Girls' team was number one at the 1995 Worlds.*

her. Williams turned just in time to take a direct hit to the bridge of the nose. With blood still trickling from her nostrils, Williams appealed to her coach to leave her in the ball game.

With the medical staff's o.k., Williams stayed in and struck out 17 consecutive batters to give the USA an important 1-0 win.

Following the game, Williams made a trip to the hospital where it was confirmed that her nose had in fact been broken.

At age 17, Christa Williams was already well on her way to earning a spot among the sport's legends and perhaps a role in leading softball forward in the years to follow.

At the 1995 U.S. Olympic Festival, the world watched as 60 of the nation's best put it on the line as team selection members watched every move. No one had to be reminded that just one month later, the final Olympic cut would be made in Oklahoma City. The competition at the Festival had never been more intense as each player instinctively knew that they were not only competing against the best in the game but for their survival as an Olympic contender.

It was a Festival that brought unprecedented visibility to the sport. Features on the 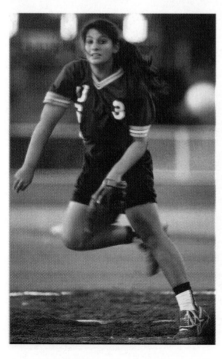 team and its players began to appear in such important publications as *USA Today*, the *New York Times*, the *St. Louis Post-Dispatch*, the *Philadelphia Enquirer*, the *Dallas Morning News* and many others. It seemed as if the whole world had instantly discovered the athletes of USA Softball and were straining for a closer look.

Although unspoken, the players were desperately seeking public acknowledgment of their achievements. The players struggled with the issue of why the greatness of their achievements had been ignored by so many for so long. It was a question in which the players were hard pressed to find answers.

There were those who could see the story unfolding here including *USA Today* Olympic editor Janice Lloyd who led the way with national stories on the team, Dr. Dot and then climbed out on a limb by making an assignment to feature a 17-year old Olympic hopeful named Christa Williams. Major pieces by Jere Longman of the *New York Times*, Mark McDonald of the *Dallas Morning News*, Debbie Becker of *USA Today*, Mike DeArmond of the *Kansas City Star*, Bill Buchalter of the *Orlando Sentinel* and Johnny Ludden of the *Washington*

Post opened the door.

The visibility certainly didn't hurt players such as Dot Richardson, who was selected to be the women's torch lighter at the gala opening ceremonies, or Christa Williams, who received the Mary Lou Retton Award at the Festival's close.

. . . .

RIGHT: *Opening ceremonies at the last U.S. Olympic Festival in 1995 at Mile High Stadium in Denver.*

OPPOSITE PAGE: *Teen phenom Christa Williams, 17, proves she can play with the best by producing one of the top pitching performances at her debut Festival.*
Photos © 1994 Arlan Flax/Alfa Photography

Then there was Superball '95 in Columbus, Georgia, site of the 1996 Olympic softball competition. Six of the eight-team field that would compete in the Olympics in 1996 assembled August 3-6 in the sport's only warm-up to the Games. Among the USA's competitors were China, Chinese Taipei, Japan, Australia and Puerto Rico.

There were some concerns for the USA in the event. Injuries plagued USA icons Michele Granger, Dot Richardson and Sheila Cornell. Granger's physical condition had been a concern since she had complained of soreness in her pitching shoulder following the Canada Cup earlier that season. It was feared that her playing schedule and strenuous personal workout regimen had taken its toll. It was not the type of injury that any Olympic hopeful would welcome just a month prior to the final selection camp.

Medical reports prior to the competition had listed Granger as healthy and on the mend. However, there was a substantial difference between pitching in practice and pitching against top international competition. Superball '95 would give Granger and the team medical staff their best evaluation of her progress.

Granger's only start came in the USA's third game of the competition against China. Granger looked strong through five innings posting an impressive 11 strikeouts and no walks. However, Granger's comeback remained incomplete as she was relieved in the sixth by Dee Dee Weiman after reporting recurring pain in her shoulder.

The test, although still not conclusive, indicated that Granger was still able to deliver and that the prognosis of full recovery was probable, provided the shoulder was given time to rest and continue the healing process. Granger could only hope that the selection committee took a similar view of her situation.

Weiman, for the record, followed with an excellent, if flawed, performance, giving up only two hits in four innings. However, one hit will be remembered as the one that found its way into the right field bleachers and ended the USA's legendary winning streak at 106-0. China's 1-0 win over the USA also gave everyone in attendance their first confirmation of just how strong the Olympic field in 1996 would likely become.

Richardson remained in the line-up despite struggling with a demoralizing and aggravating groin pull sustained in competition at the U.S. Olympic Festival. Cornell played sparingly after colliding with catcher Michelle Gromacki and a fence during pursuit of a foul tip along the first base line. These ailments created concern in the minds of two of the sport's most productive veterans,

who at the age of 34 each, were making their challenge against a much younger field of competitors. Nagging injuries would not enhance their ability to make the team and they knew it.

Despite the loss to China, the USA remained the team to beat, racking up wins over Chinese Taipei, 6-0; Australia, 3-0; Puerto Rico, 7-0; and Japan, 1-0. The USA then had to face China again for the gold medal.

In the final against China, the USA struck early and regularly starting with a second inning home run into the right field cheap

seats by rising power hitter Kim Maher. Maher, although not a newcomer to elite softball, became

. . . .

ABOVE: *Kim Maher takes it home in final against China in Superball '95.*

LEFT: *Catcher Michele Gromacki in conference with Michele Smith.*

OPPOSITE PAGE (FAR LEFT): *Dot grimaces as she battles injury at Superball '95.*

OPPOSITE PAGE (LEFT): *Dee Dee Weiman letting it fly at Superball '95.*
All photos on these pages courtesy of USA Softball/Doug Hoke

a serious Olympic contender following her record breaking performance at the 1994 ASA Women's Major National Championship in which she broke a two-decade old national record for most home runs with five. Power hitting/power pitching was certainly a tantalizing combination that the selection committee would be enticed to explore further.

Richardson followed with an RBI single in the second to score Michele Smith and the rout was on.

The USA added two runs in the third, a Shelly Stokes home run in the fourth, two more runs in the fifth and a final score in the eighth to win 8-0. USA pitcher Lisa Fernandez went the distance delivering 10 strikeouts, no walks and one hit to reassert herself as perhaps the top all-around player in the world. The USA had made their statement to China and the rest of the field, the USA remained the favorite for Olympic gold.

The Superball event also gave the USA team their first glimpse of the community of Columbus, Georgia which would host the Games in 1996. Columbus, although over 100 miles outside of the Olympic hub of Atlanta, earned the respect of the team and the USA Softball staff by their demonstrated affection for the sport and its athletes. This was a community that loved the players as much as the players loved the prospects of being there for the Olympics. It was a perfect match: USA Softball and Columbus, Georgia, both on the threshold of softball history.

OPPOSITE PAGE:
ABOVE: *Michele Smith running the bases.*
LEFT: *Lisa Fernandez was lethal in the final at Superball '95.*
RIGHT: *Columbus '96 chief Carmen Cavezza offers his congratulations at the medal ceremony at Superball '95.*

THIS PAGE: SUPERBALL '95 REMEMBERED
TOP: (FROM LEFT TO RIGHT) *Trish Popowski, Martha O'Kelley, Coach Raymond makes his point, Laura Berg was spectacular in the field.*
MIDDLE: *Michele Smith, Dot Richardson hoists the flag, Kim Maher at Columbus, and WTVM-9 Sports director, Dave Platta.*
BOTTOM: *The USA in triumph, Laura Berg receives her medal from Don Porter, Then ASA president Wayne Myers offers congratulations to head coach.*

All photos on these pages courtesy of USA Softball/Doug Hoke

Inevitably the process led to one final Olympic Selection Camp on Labor Day weekend 1995 in Oklahoma City.

Tired and stretched physically and emotionally, the final field of 67 players met in Oklahoma City for their last evaluation at the 1995 USA Softball Olympic Team Camp.

The great significance of the moment was not lost on any of the attendees. Everyone knew that by week's end, 15 would advance to the

Olympics, the rest would go home. For some, there would likely be another Olympic tryout for them sometime down the road. A long three-year process was behind them, a process that would probably better their chances for making teams in 2000 and 2004. But for others, their Olympic dreams would die here. There would be no Olympics for them. The contributions they had made to the sport would remain, but their dreams of standing on the Olympic podium had vanished.

Dot Richardson, 34, knew too well what this moment meant and what was at stake. At

made and followed perhaps the most intense and grueling 12-month final stretch ever for America's softball athletes and for the seven member national selection committee. The strains of 36 months of travel and evaluation were evident on them also.

One of the committee members, Kathy Arendsen, was a former player who once had Olympic dreams of her own. "It will be tough not being on the field in 1996. Somehow most

the age of 13, Dot had dreamed of someday being an Olympian. She saw her prospects of fulfilling her dream diminish when the Olympics passed the sport by repeatedly.

"There was a sense of pride, but also of fear. What would it feel like to make or not make this team?" Richardson asked herself.

"We're on the brink of becoming part of history. It's been the dream of all of us since we were little girls to play in the Olympics for the USA," Richardson said.

The selection of the team was among the most difficult decisions the sport had ever

ABOVE: *Coach Raymond and ASA Director of Operations Tim O'Toole.*

ABOVE LEFT: *Dot Richardson at the 1995 Olympic Team Camp.*

OPPOSITE PAGE (TOP LEFT): *Players gather at the 1995 Olympic Team Camp.*

OPPOSITE PAGE (BOTTOM LEFT): *Debbie Doom pitching.*

OPPOSITE PAGE (BOTTOM RIGHT): *Preparing to board.*

All photos on these pages courtesy of USA Softball/Doug Hoke

That's how I felt my Freshman year at Bloom. How would my friends feel if I didn't make the Team?

of us hoped that it would someday happen to us also. This team will represent the USA and softball well and I'll be there to support them," she said. Many other veteran softball athletes echoed the sentiment.

. . . .

TOP TO BOTTOM (LEFT TO RIGHT): *Susie Gaw and fans; Susie Parra; Fernandez and public; Pat Dufficy rounding the bases; Laura Berg goes up in centerfield; Veteran Michele Smith; Lori Harrigan pitching; Heather Compton; Christa Williams; Cheri Kempf; DeeDee Weiman; Dani Tyler with play at second; Catcher Karen Sanchelli taking it in stride; Martha O'Kelley in the dirt; Coach Weekly counsels player.*

BACKGROUND: *Field shot.*

All photos on these pages courtesy of USA Softball/Doug Hoke

The 15-member team was publicly announced in a press conference September 4th at the Marriott Hotel in Oklahoma City completing a selection cycle that had for over three years searched the

nation in hopes of fielding the best possible team to represent the USA in the Olympics.

Named to USA Softball's first Olympic team were Laura Berg of Santa Fe Springs,

Rookie" center- fielder.

California; Gillian Boxx of Torrance, California; Sheila Cornell of Diamond Bar, California; Lisa Fernandez of Long Beach, California; Michele Granger of Anchorage, Alaska; Lori Harrigan of Las Vegas, Nevada; Dionna Harris of Wilmington, Delaware; Kim Maher of Fresno, California; Leah O'Brien of Chino, California; Dot Richardson of Orlando, Florida; Julie Smith of Glendora, California; Michele Smith of Califon, New Jersey; Shelly Stokes of Carmichael, California; Dani Tyler of Des Moines, Iowa; and Christa Williams of Houston, Texas.

Five alternates were also named including Jennifer McFalls of Grand Prairie, Texas;

Barbara Jordan of Huntington Beach, California; Martha O'Kelley of Las Vegas, California; Michelle Venturella of South Holland, Illinois; and Dee Dee Weiman of Los Angeles, California. Weiman later withdrew and was replaced with Jennifer Brundage of Irvine, California.

The Olympic team was first announced to the players at their hotel in the early hours of September 4th. Each of the players handled the decision differently, all with great emotion.

"None of us got much sleep that night. I finally dozed off about 4 a.m. only to be

How I feel before a game.

LEFT: *Veteran Julie Smith extends thanks flanked by Don Porter and ASA President Wayne Myers.*

OPPOSITE PAGE (TOP LEFT): *Ron Babb, Director of Public Information & Media conducting press conference.*

OPPOSITE PAGE (TOP RIGHT): *Coaches Ralph Weekly, Margie Wright and Ralph Raymond.*

OPPOSITE PAGE (BOTTOM): *Porter surrounded by his Olympians.*

OPPOSITE PAGE (INSET): *Joe Szombathy of Coca-Cola USA, USA Softball's National Team Sponsor.*
All photos on these pages courtesy of USA Softball/Doug Hoke

awakened by Dot Richardson and Lisa Fernandez. Dot was standing on the bed with the list in her hand. Several of my younger teammates were also in the room," Christa Williams said. "And, the 1996 USA Softball Olympic Team is...Laura Berg," Richardson said, pausing after each name to relish the moment.

"She was reading the names slowly, alphabetically and my name started with 'W'. I thought I was going to burst," Williams said. The list got to Richardson and everyone cheered, and finally, Williams. "I wept for joy," she said.

"I can't explain how I felt when I saw my name on the list. All of the emotions I have felt in a lifetime came rushing in on me at the same time," Richardson said.

"When I look back on my career, I realize that this day almost didn't happen for me. If someone had not made room for a 10-year-old kid, there would be no Dot Richardson as an Olympian."

In the press conference that followed that morning, Richardson took time to pay homage to those who went before and those who were not selected.

After beating Cal At States Sophomore year.

"All of the players who competed for these spots over the last 2½ years and all those who went before and prepared the way, remain a part of this team. Without their contributions to the sport and to myself as a player, the sport would not have the opportunity to play in the Olympics, and as a player I would not be standing here today.

"For the past two decades, I have been a part of something bigger than myself. We are a part of a team that has been around for generations. A team that will live on in the lives of athletes long after our playing days are over," Richardson said.

With softball's first Olympic team selected, the important process of preparing the team for their appointment with destiny was only beginning.

. . . .

ABOVE: *Dani Tyler and Christa Williams fielding questions.*

LEFT: *Dionna Harris, Kim Maher, Leah O'Brien and Dot Richardson.*

OPPOSITE PAGE (TOP): *A joyful Leah O'Brien.*

OPPOSITE PAGE (BOTTOM): *Fernandez's tearful comments.*
All photos on these pages courtesy of USA Softball/Doug Hoke

LAURA
BERG

GILLIAN
BOXX

SHEILA
CORNELL

LORI
HARRIGAN

DIONNA
HARRIS

KIM
MAHER

JULIE
SMITH

MICHELE
SMITH

SHELLY
STOKES

HEAD COACH
RALPH RAYMOND

ASSISTANT COACH
RALPH WEEKLY

ASSISTANT COACH
MARGIE WRIGHT

LISA
FERNANDEZ

MICHELE
GRANGER

LEAH
O'BRIEN

DOT
RICHARDSON

DANI
TYLER

CHRISTA
WILLIAMS

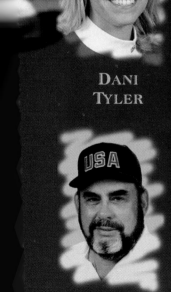

TEAM LEADER
RONNIE ISHAM

5
AMERICA'S
TEAM

Photos courtesy of USA Softball

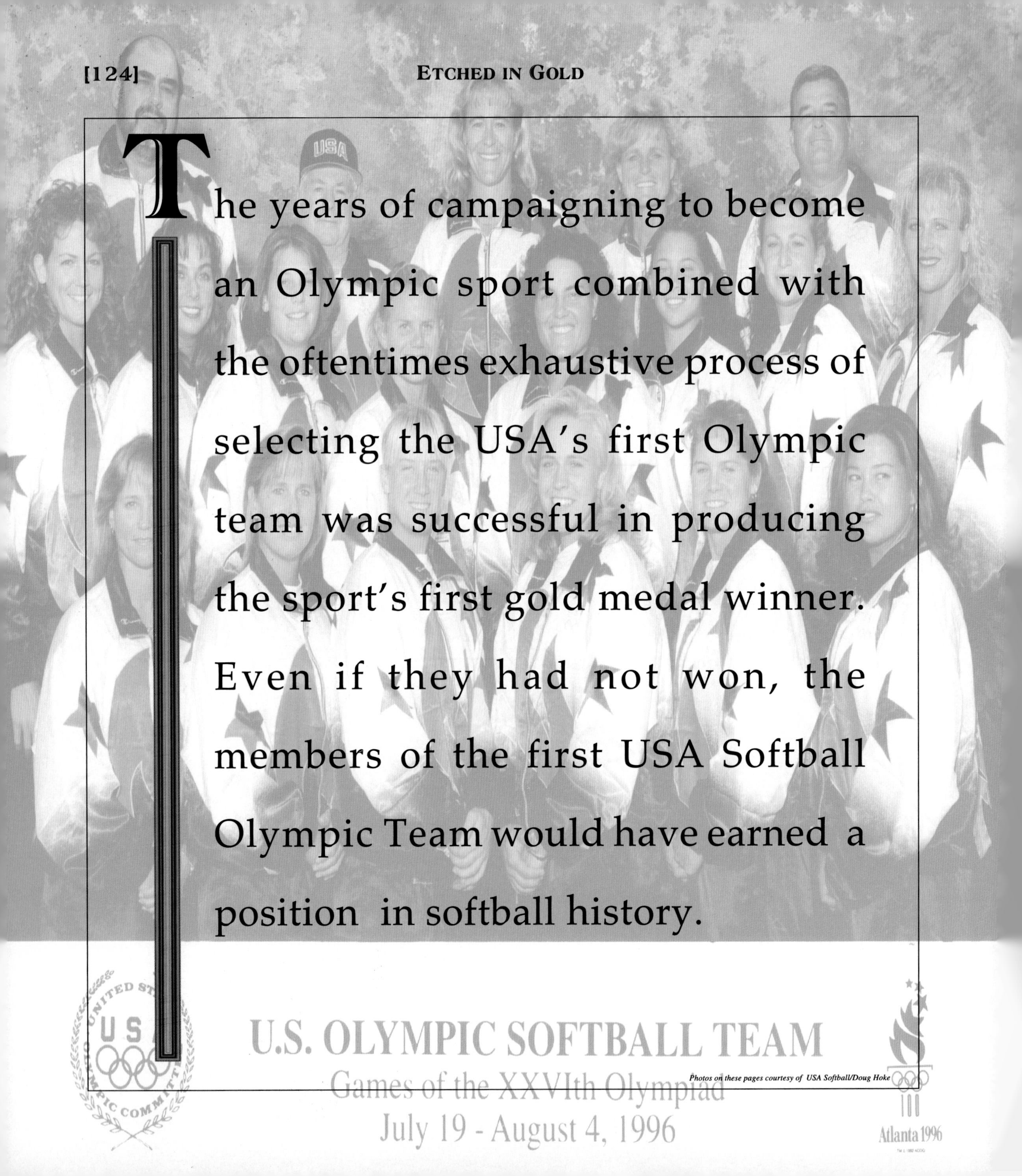

The years of campaigning to become an Olympic sport combined with the oftentimes exhaustive process of selecting the USA's first Olympic team was successful in producing the sport's first gold medal winner. Even if they had not won, the members of the first USA Softball Olympic Team would have earned a position in softball history.

U.S. OLYMPIC SOFTBALL TEAM
Games of the XXVIth Olympiad
July 19 - August 4, 1996

Photos on these pages courtesy of USA Softball/Doug Hoke

Atlanta 1996

LAURA BERG

Many have called Laura Berg the best outfield prospect to play the game this decade. Her catlike heroics in chasing down almost sure hits and turning them into routine outs convince all who have seen her in action.

Berg, although soft spoken, has a propensity for the big play. In the 1994 ISF World Championships in Canada, China threatened in the gold medal game. With a runner on second base, the Chinese managed what appeared to be the go-ahead hit, a shot through the gap that careened off the center field fence. Berg, seemingly undaunted by the challenge, was there in an instant, scooping up the ball and producing a one-hop strike to the plate in time to pick off the runner. The play single-handedly stalled the Chinese threat and shifted the game's momentum back to the USA.

Berg produced similar heroics in the Olympics including the USA's second game against the Netherlands. USA pitcher Christa Williams struck out the first batter she faced before Gerardina Reinen reached base on an error by Dot Richardson and was advanced to second on a ground out. With a runner on second and two outs, Perta Beek appeared to have produced an RBI hit to center until Berg made a spectacular, fully-extended diving catch to end the inning and the Netherlands scoring threat. The catch secured Williams' 9-0 shutout performance in her Olympic debut.

Berg owns the outfield and is among the stingiest defensive players in the world. Her ability to react in a split second and

run down long balls, sometimes snatching them just before they exit the outfield fence, makes her one of the most exciting players to watch. Her quickness on the base paths and her proven ability to stretch her hits into extra bases make her a threat every time she steps up to the plate.

Berg has been competing in athletics most of her life, earning 11 varsity letters in three sports at Santa Fe High School, four each in softball and basketball and three in volleyball. Even as a youth in the ASA Junior Olympic Program, Berg showed her prowess leading the Orange County Batbusters to the ASA Girls' 18-Under National Championship title in 1992 and runner-up finishes in 1989, 1991 and 1993. Collegiately at Fresno State University, Berg has received numerous All-Conference, All-Region and All-American honors.

As one of Fresno State's most prolific performers, Berg holds the all-time single season record for triples (11) and runs (25). In 1995, she led the team in doubles (13), extra base hits (25) and stolen bases (11). She completed the

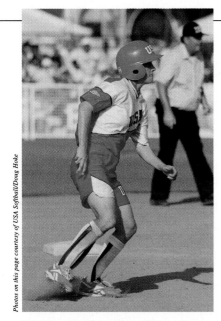

1995 season batting .425 and was named to the All-West, All-WAC and All-American teams. She had not made a fielding error in 99 consecutive games at Fresno State through the 1995 season.

In her international debut at the ISF World Championships, Berg also distinguished herself as one of the team's most consistent hitters producing five hits, scoring four times and batting .385.

Berg also won a gold medal in 1995 while competing on the USA team at Superball '95 in Columbus, Georgia. In the semi-final against Japan, Berg drove in the winning run in the third inning after Michelle Gromacki had walked and stolen second. Berg followed with a double into the center field fence that scored Gromacki and gave the

USA a 1-0 lead that earned their spot in the gold medal game.

At the Olympics, Berg distinguished herself batting .273 with six hits including a double and scoring twice, including a decisive run against China in the final. In the third inning of the final, Berg singled to leadoff the inning. Dot Richardson followed with the big blow that cleared the right field fence putting the USA up 2-

0, a lead they never relinquished. Few will forget Berg and Richardson's triumphant trek to home.

Berg also had one of the highest on-base percentages of the team at .393, likely aided by the fact that she reached base five times after being hit by a pitch, a tournament record.

GILLIAN BOXX

Although they did not play together in college, Gillian Boxx and Olympic teammate Michele Granger are undisputably the most successful softball players to have ever attended the University of California-Berkeley. When they did team up at the 1996 Olympics, they had the distinction of playing in softball's first Olympic game, a 10-0 blow-out of Puerto Rico, and in the gold medal game against China, which the USA won 3-1.

In the Olympics, Boxx played in 44.2 innings and posted a perfect 1.000 fielding percentage. She also contributed four hits and two runs, including a double, batted .250 and produced three RBI.

In the USA's first game against Puerto Rico, Boxx delivered two hits including a bases-loaded single in the bottom of the third inning to score teammates Kim Maher and Sheila Cornell to give the USA a 5-0 lead.

In an important game against Canada and with the score knotted at 2-2, Boxx produced a double to lead off the seventh inning. Dionna Harris was brought in as a pinch runner for Boxx and later scored on a passed ball to give the USA the lead for good at 3-2. The USA scored once more in the inning and defeated a tough Canadian team 4-2.

Like many of her teammates, Boxx was successful early in her career at South High School in Torrance, California where she batted .427 as a senior with a .787 slugging percentage. She also produced five home runs, 24 RBI and 16 stolen bases.

Photos on this page courtesy of USA Softball/Doug Hoke

Boxx continued her storied career at Berkeley, where she rewrote their record books with seven career and five season school records including at-bats (742), runs (156), hits (274), doubles (44), RBI (146), total bases (372) and walks (103). She completed her college days in 1995 with a .369 batting average and four NCAA All-American selections. She was also named to the All-Pac10 first team in 1993, 1994 and 1995.

Her entry into the international sports arena came in 1994 as a member of the USA team that won their third consecutive ISF World Championship gold medal in Canada. In that debut, Boxx

batted .800 with four hits and scored three times.

A second gold medal followed at the 1995 Pan American Qualifier in Guatemala where she contributed nine hits, seven RBI and six runs. Boxx was already displaying her importance on defense with a perfect performance behind the plate in Guatemala (1.000).

Boxx once stated that she tried to "imagine what it would be like to make the first Olympic team and win the gold medal." Now she knows.

SHEILA CORNELL

At the age of 34, Sheila Cornell may be playing the best softball of her career. And, when you talk about Sheila Cornell's career that is a big statement.

When Cornell steps up to the plate you can almost hear a collective sigh from her opponents, with good reason. Cornell is among the most dangerous long-ball hitters to have ever worn the USA Softball uniform. For example, at the 1994 ISF World Championships

Some day, so will I. [handwritten]

in Canada, Cornell batted .357 with 10 hits, including two home runs. The following year at the 1995 Pan American Games in Argentina she led the team with a .581 batting average, producing 18 hits and three doubles and creating mayhem for the USA's opponents each time she approached the plate.

Cornell carried her impressive record into the Olympics in 1996 and became one of the major

forces behind the USA's successful run. Cornell batted .393 and led the team in hits (11), RBI (9), total bases (22), and slugging percentage (.786). She tied teammate Dot Richardson for most doubles (2) and home runs (3) *and* contributed 51 putouts from her position at first base.

Cornell began her offensive run in game one of the Olympics against Puerto Rico with a hit in the bottom of the third to load the

bases. She later scored to give the USA a 4-0 lead and then doubled in the bottom of the sixth with Lisa Fernandez on base to push the score to 7-0.

Cornell delivered her first home run of the competition in game two against the Netherlands in the bottom of the fourth inning, also scoring teammates Dani Tyler and Kim Maher. She also contributed a hit in the second, scored twice and produced three RBI.

The second home run came in the USA's win over Chinese Taipei. With a 2-0 lead heading into the bottom of the third, Cornell hit a deep ball into the left field bleachers scoring Kim Maher and insuring the USA's 4-0 victory.

Cornell's third and final home run of the competition came in a tightly contested game against China. In the top of the sixth inning, China trailed the USA by a

run before producing a two-run homer to grab the lead at 2-1. In the bottom of the sixth, Kim Maher of the USA reached on a walk and Cornell cranked a two-run blast into the left center field seats to give the USA a 3-2 win. The win allowed the USA to finish in first place in the round robin portion of the competition.

In the semi-final game against China, Cornell again delivered the winning blow, this time in the 10th inning. With the score tied at 0-0, Dot Richardson was placed on second to start the inning via the international tie breaker rule. The USA loaded the bases and Cornell delivered the RBI single to score Richardson and secure the win. The 1-0 win was the second in a row over China and earned the USA their spot in the gold medal final.

An imposing figure at 5'10", Cornell almost dares her

opponents to send a ball toward her position at first. When someone does take up the challenge, she quickly extinguishes

Photos on these pages courtesy of USA Softball/Doug Hoke

their hopes with flawless defensive play.

Cornell remains the most decorated player to have ever worn the red, white and blue. She began her legendary medal run in 1983, taking a silver at the Pan American Games in Venezuela. From that championship forward, Cornell has managed nine straight gold medals including the ISF World Championships in 1990 and 1994, the Pan American Games in 1987, 1991 and 1995 and the 1996 Olympic Games.

Nationally, Cornell has been named an ASA All-American numerous times and has twice led the ASA Women's Major National Championships in home runs.

Collegiately, Cornell was a member of the UCLA (NCAA) National Championship teams in 1982 and 1984.

LISA FERNANDEZ

No one in the sport of softball plays with more intensity, heart and resolve to win than Lisa Fernandez, as demonstrated by her inspiring performance in the 1996 Olympic Games.

Fernandez's performance was both inspirational and gut-wrenching. In the USA's round robin game against Australia, Fernandez was perfect. Through seven complete innings, Fernandez had pitched a perfect game, retiring 12 batters on

strikes. It was a game that should have been recorded as the first perfect game in Olympic history. It was not to be.

The USA had taken a 1-0 lead in the fifth inning when Dani Tyler hit a pitch into the seventh row of the center field bleachers. In her exuberance, Tyler forgot to touch home plate and the Australians appealed and Tyler was called out and the run disallowed. Gone in an instant were Tyler's home run and Fernandez's perfect game.

Fernandez continued her perfect game into the bottom of the tenth. The USA had scored in the top of the inning on an RBI single by Sheila Cornell to lead 1-0. With a 1-0 lead and showing no signs of letting up, Fernandez appeared to have the game under control. Then it all came tumbling down. With two outs and two strikes on Joanne Brown of Australia, Fernandez delivered perhaps her only imperfect pitch of the game, a riseball that flattened out slightly as it crossed the plate. With nothing to lose, Brown took a huge cut and drove the ball into the centerfield bleachers, stunning a partisan USA crowd who thought this one was in the record books. Fernandez, who had pitched the USA's finest game of the Olympics, was devastated.

There was little time for remorse with the USA facing China as its next opponent and needing a win to secure its position as leader after the round robin. Fernandez, perhaps the toughest mental warrior in the sport, put the loss behind her and pressed on.

The USA won their round robin game against China 3-2 and moved on to a rematch in the first game of the semi-finals. Just two days after Fernandez's gut-wrenching loss, she was back in the circle battling the USA's toughest challenge in a

I can prove this wrong. Dare Me?

wounded and hungry China. Fernandez met the challenge with 13 strikeouts in a three-hit, 10-inning, 1-0 shutout win that advanced the USA to the gold medal game.

In the gold medal final, the USA faced the challenge of defeating China for the third consecutive time. Teammate Michele Granger got the start for the USA and led 3-0 through five innings, thanks to a big third inning which included a two-run homer by Dot Richardson. However, in the top of the sixth China began a rally with a single and a double to left. With two outs and two runners on, Fernandez came in to close out the contest. China scored on a passed ball before Fernandez closed out the side with a strikeout of Ying Wang.

China's lead-off batter grounded

out in the top of the seventh and Fernandez followed with consecutive strikeouts of their next two batters to secure the win and claim the USA's first Olympic gold medal.

Fernandez completed the competition with a win, a loss and a save and lead the team in strikeouts (31) and innings pitched (21).

Fernandez started all nine games for the USA. When she was not in the circle she was at home on third and produced a perfect fielding percentage of 1.000 in the competition. She also contributed eight hits, five runs, five RBI and batted .393, third highest on the team.

Fernandez also demonstrated her power with a three-RBI home run in the sixth inning against Japan to give the USA a commanding 6-1 lead.

Even with years ahead of her, Fernandez has already had a storied international career. In the final against China in Superball '95 in Columbus, Georgia, Fernandez was snorting fire on every pitch and building confidence with every completed inning. Her one-hit performance led a 12-hit, 8-run USA attack that defeated China and served notice to anyone in view that the USA was ready to take on all comers.

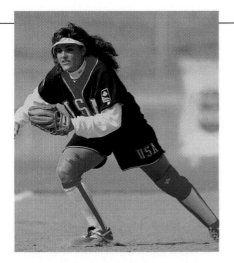

Fernandez's energy is contagious and her teammates understand that when she is on the mound they are expected to play their best, and most of all, they are expected to win. Fernandez's intensity came early. "Losing goes deep for me, it goes right to my heart, my dignity." She is harder on herself than she is on her teammates, however, and is reputed to have the best work ethic in the sport, based largely on her belief that game mistakes are attributed directly to being unprepared. "It's traumatic to lose when you have given 150 percent."

Fernandez can credit at least a portion of her mental toughness and resiliency to her parents. Before the Bay of Pigs invasion, father Tony played semi-pro baseball in Cuba before fleeing to the U.S. in 1962, and mother Emilia became an inspirational force behind her daughter, encouraging her to always "go for what you want."

Fernandez recalls Emilia's important counsel following a traumatic conversation with her coach early in her career. The coach had told Fernandez that her arms were too short to play softball, a critique that Fernandez took perhaps more deeply than the coach expected. After listening to a sobbing Fernandez, mom Emilia explained an important life principle that Lisa took to heart. "Others can try to tell you what you can and cannot do in life, but that doesn't mean you have to listen to it," she said. Fernandez has refused to listen to any banter about her limitations on or off the field since.

Fernandez remains among the nation's most recognizable stars, largely because of the Olympics and her bigger-than-life career at UCLA. In college, Fernandez routinely did the impossible and then challenged herself to do more. In her senior season at UCLA, she not only led the nation in ERA (0.25) but also in batting average at .510, a record that will likely remain on the books for some time.

By the time she had completed her run at UCLA she had led her team to two national titles and was selected to four NCAA All-America teams. She compiled a career 93-7 record at UCLA, batted .382 and holds career records for

Wow, that really hits home.

singles (225), runs scored (142), walks (85), hits (287), most wins (93), winning percentage (.930) and no-hitters (11). She also broke the NCAA all-time winning percentage record (.930).

Internationally, Fernandez has put gold around her neck at such competitions as the 1990 and 1994 ISF World Championships, the 1992 Challenger Cup in Beijing, the 1993 Intercontinental Cup in Holland, the 1994 South Pacific Classic in Australia, the 1995 Pan American Games Qualifier in Guatemala, Superball '95 in Columbus, Georgia and the 1996 Olympic Games.

MICHELE GRANGER

Since Michele Granger's international debut at the age of 16, the legend that has surrounded the USA's most prolific strikeout machine has continued to grow. Reputedly the world's fastest thrower, Granger can bring the heat at a level that intimidates not only the batter but everyone in close proximity of her target.

In 1996, Granger added to her resumé by becoming the first USA

pitcher to start in the Olympic Games. In game one against Puerto Rico, Granger pitched a two-hitter, stringing together 10 strikeouts enroute to an easy 10-0 debut for the USA in the Olympics.

Granger was sharp against Puerto Rico, allowing no base runners from the fourth inning forward. Her teammates gave the competition their first look at the USA's powerful offensive attack, producing 10 runs on 13 hits.

In the USA's fifth game against Canada, Granger retired seven batters through the top of the fourth inning and was riding a 2-0 USA lead into the bottom of the fifth when Canada began their move scoring two runs on a single by rightfielder Kara McGaw, a triple by centerfielder Pauline Maurice

and an RBI single by first baseman Carmelina Vairo. With the score knotted at 2-2 and Granger suddenly running on empty, 18-year-old rookie Christa Williams came in and contributed a gutsy performance by closing out the inning with two strikeouts. Granger, obviously disappointed by her rapid change of fortune, would find her way back into the spotlight later in the competition.

Known for her easy California, laid-back style, Granger is a non-assuming charmer. Her amusing anecdotes of her life travels are both endearing and revealing.

For example, while competing for a spot on the team, this California girl followed her attorney husband to the ends of the earth so that he could take advantage of an opportunity to work with an Alaskan Supreme Court Justice. The move to the icy

confines of Alaska presented more than its share of challenges for a California softball pitcher with her sights set on making her sport's first Olympic team. "When you train for the Olympics in Alaska you have to be creative." Granger has pitched in freight warehouses, into nets in her garage and even a church.

"A Protestant church allowed me to pitch in their basement. They didn't even seem to mind that I was Catholic and that I was putting holes in their walls," she said.

Granger has been a prolific performer from her early days, pitching the USA to a gold medal at the 1986 ISF World Championships at the age of 16 and following with a gold medal at the 1987 Jr. Girls' World Championship. She has the distinction of being the only player in history to compete in the ISF Jr. Girls' World Championship, the U.S. Olympic Festival, the Pan American Games and the ASA Women's Major National Championships in the same year (1987).

In college, Granger put the University of California-Berkeley on the softball map, setting 20 of 22 school records and six NCAA records including all-time strikeout leader.

Sometimes reserved on the surface, Granger does know how to make her point. Granger recalls one game in which she had requested a new ball from the umpire only to be refused. Her next pitch was over the backstop and into the parking lot. The umpire cautioned her against a repeat and Granger got her new ball.

In international play, Granger's reputation for throwing the heat is legendary. She is also inclined to occasionally let one fly just so the

Sucker!

opposing batters can see what they are up against. One 75 m.p.h. riseball, up and into the backstop, is enough for most to get the picture.

Granger led the USA to gold medals in the 1986 and 1994 ISF World Championship, the 1987 ISF Jr. Girls' World Championship, the 1991 and 1995 Pan American Games, the 1994 South Pacific Classic and Superball '95.

At the Pan American Games in 1995, Granger led the team with four wins (4-0) and a perfect 0.00 ERA. She also produced an eye popping 57 strikeouts to lead the tournament and gave up only three hits in 24 innings pitched. Granger's biggest wins at the Pan Ams included a pair of shutouts against a talented and upset-bent Cuban team. In the USA's ninth game of the event, Granger extinguished the threat by fanning 19 batters and allowing only two hits to defeat Cuba 2-0 and extend the USA's unbeaten streak in the competition to 9-0.

Ironically, Granger would later face Cuba in a rematch during the playoffs and deliver a remarkable perfect game, striking out 16 batters in a 5-0 win that sent the USA into the gold medal game. It was Granger's fourth win in the competition and her ninth in

three Pan American Games.

There was considerable debate among softball officinados on who would get the first and last start in the Olympic Games. Granger remarkably got both. In the gold medal final against China, Granger came out firing, not allowing a run through five complete innings and retiring eight batters on strikes. Thanks to an explosive three-run third inning for the USA, Granger appeared to be shifting into overdrive and heading for home.

However, China was not ready to call it a day yet and in the top of the sixth managed runners at second and third with two outs. With too much at stake to risk a rally, USA head coach Ralph Raymond made the percentage call and relieved Granger with Lisa Fernandez who retired the side and closed out the win.

Granger's debut in the Olympics had been significant as she ended the series with two wins, an 0.87 ERA, a team leading 25 strikeouts, starts in the first and final game of the Olympics, and a gold medal. She also had a surprise announcement for her teammates. She was two months pregnant and headed home to California to start a family with her husband John.

LORI HARRIGAN

Lori Harrigan may well be the best "unknown" pitcher in the world. Unknown perhaps to the general public, but highly respected and highly regarded by every player who swings a bat in international competition.

In 1994, Lori Harrigan led the USA Softball Women's National Team to their third consecutive ISF World Championship title by shutting out China 6-0 in the gold

medal final. It was Harrigan's fifth gold medal for the USA since her inaugural international competition at the 1992 Challenger Cup in Beijing.

At the 1994 World Championships, China threatened early. With a runner on second, China delivered a rope to center but teammate Laura Berg responded, nailing the runner at the plate. Harrigan responded also, slamming the door on the challenger in a near flawless pitching performance the remainder of the game. Because of her title game performance, many, including China, came into the Olympic Games believing that Harrigan was the best in the West.

Harrigan's performance in the Olympics only reinforced the perception. Although Harrigan received only one start in the Games, she made the most of her moment delivering a 4-0 shutout win over a scrappy team from Chinese Taipei. Southpaw Harrigan's control of the game was so exact that no runner reached second base during the contest. The only hits surrendered during the game were scattered in the second and sixth innings and Chinese Taipei's upset hopes were quickly snuffed out by Harrigan riseballs and change-ups.

Harrigan's Olympic debut contributed a two-hit shutout with five strikeouts and seven innings of 0.00 ERA softball.

Harrigan began her playing days on the softball fields of Anaheim, CA and shared her moments of early glory as a member of the Magnolia High School softball team. At Magnolia, Lori earned seven varsity letters -- four in softball, three in volleyball and was named league MVP in

softball during her sophomore, junior and senior seasons.

Harrigan has the skills to dominate a contest as demonstrated in her college days at the University of Nevada-Las Vegas. Harrigan made a difference from the beginning at UNLV, leading the team in batting average at .311 her freshman year and shattering virtually every single-season UNLV pitching standard.

During her collegiate career, she pitched the Lady Rebels to three

NCAA regional appearances and two berths in the NCAA Women's College World Series. Harrigan finished at UNLV setting all-time team records for most wins (83), saves (7), strikeouts (725), ERA (0.77), complete games (123), shutouts (53) and innings pitched (1,034.6).

At the 1995 Pan American Games, Harrigan was again impressive securing important wins over Canada (2-0) and Argentina (11-0) and posting a perfect 0.00 ERA with 17 strikeouts in 12 innings pitched.

Internationally, Harrigan has brought home USA gold at the 1992 Challenger Cup in China, the 1993 Intercontinental Cup in Holland, the 1994 South Pacific Classic in Sydney, Australia, the 1994 ISF Women's World Championship in St. John's, Newfoundland, Canada, the 1995 Pan American Games in Argentina and now the biggest of them all, the 1996 Olympic Games.

DIONNA HARRIS

One has to marvel at the achievement of making softball's first-ever Olympic team. Especially if the player in

Photos on these pages courtesy of USA Softball/Doug Hoke

Harris' selection to the USA Olympic team's sweet-15 still came as a surprise to some, but it was a choice that was proven a solid one in competition. Harris responded to the challenge by pounding out nine hits and leading the team in batting average in both the round robin (.500) and through the medal rounds (.409). Even after the competition had concluded, there were few who recognized the magnitude of her achievement.

Harris received her first Olympic start in game two against the Netherlands and quickly made her presence known, delivering three hits in three at-bats and scoring twice. In her first Olympic game, Harris was batting a perfect 1.000.

Harris extended her perfect batting streak into the next game against Japan and completed the event with a team-leading .409. She was also perfect defensively throughout.

Harris grew up in Stanton, DE and played her high school ball at Delcastle Tech High School and, in the framework of four short years, developed a reputation as perhaps the finest athlete to have ever walked their hallowed halls. The school recognized her efforts in 1996 by retiring her jersey.

Growing up in Delaware doesn't provide a fast track to the Olympics, at least Olympic softball. "There were so few quality fast pitch teams in our area when I was growing up, I played slow pitch to stay in the game," she said.

Despite her lack of early recognition, Harris still managed to catch the eye of the coaching staff at Temple University. Harris helped lead Temple to an Atlantic 10

question grew up in the rural confines of a small town in Delaware playing the only softball in town -- slow pitch. No one understands the accomplishment and the challenge better than Dionna Harris.

Harris began emerging as a world class performer while representing the USA in the 1993 Intercontinental Cup in Holland. She continued to show progress at the 1994 Pan Am Qualifier in Guatemala, batting .370 with ten hits through the round robin. Although she did not have the benefit of the west coast hype and publicity that some of her future Olympic team-mates had, those who were looking closely saw that Harris was rapidly becoming a rising star in the sport.

Championship and was recognized for her efforts by being named the 1990 Temple University Player of the Year.

Harris has also built a reputation as one of the nation's finest women's players and led the 1995 ASA Women's Major Championship in batting with a .611 average.

"When I was growing up I had a dream of playing in the Olympics. But, with the challenge of competing for only a few coveted spots, there was some concern that a girl from a small rural town in the East might somehow be overlooked. But, I kept practicing and doing the things I could to keep the dream alive," she said.

Even though Harris lacked the playing opportunities of her West Coast peers, she did not lack in pure athletic ability. She was chosen for her skill in covering the outfield, running the bases and delivering the key hit when needed. She delivered big-time in all three areas.

KIM MAHER

Kim Maher is a big-play athlete with incredible power at bat and a rare touch that allows her to place her hits to fit almost any scenario.

Maher vaulted to national prominence in 1994 when she set the all-time home run record at the ASA Women's Major National Championship with five.

She has been equally impressive in her outings for the USA. In the 1995 Pan American Games in Argentina, Maher batted .375 with 12 hits and scored nine times. She was also errorless in the field.

Maher won her second USA gold medal at Superball '95. In the final in Columbus, GA, Maher started a 12-hit USA barrage with a towering blast that cleared the left field bleachers to give the USA a 1-0 lead over China. The USA buried its challenger 8-0.

Maher started off strong in the Olympics in game one against Puerto Rico, delivering two hits in four at-bats including a double in the first inning. She also produced one of the Olympic Games' most memorable moments against Japan in game three. In the bottom of the first inning, the USA had their offense in gear with a single to center by Julie Smith and a follow-up drive to rightfield by Lisa Fernandez. Maher stepped to the plate, dusted her shoes and, Bingo!, delivered a three-RBI, "big-play" rope into the left field bleachers that gave the USA a 3-0 advantage and set the course for an important 6-1 win. She completed the Olympics with seven hits, a double, a home run, three RBI and tied teammate Dot Richardson for most runs scored at seven.

Maher enjoyed a great deal of success before moving up to international competition. She won three national titles as a member of the Redding Rebels of Redding, CA., the 1993, 1994 and 1995 ASA Women's Major National Champions. She was

also a member of the ASA Girls' 18-and-Under National Championship team in 1987.

Collegiately, Maher was All-Conference in 1992, 1993 and 1994 at Fresno State University and an NCAA All-American in 1994. She was a member of the Fresno State teams that finished third at the NCAA Women's College World Series in 1991 and 1992 and fifth in 1994.

Maher's is an All-American success story. Her father, an American, met her mother while doing business in Saigon. Her parents were married and remained in Saigon until moving to California in 1971, a couple of months after Maher's birth. Maher's selection and ultimate USA gold medal victory in the Olympic Games was a storybook conclusion to her first-generation American dream. "I don't think anyone could top being on softball's first Olympic team," she said.

LEAH O'BRIEN

Leah O'Brien made the most of her international debut in the 1995 Pan American Games Qualifier, leading the team in hitting with a .513 batting average.

She followed later in 1995 with her second gold medal at Superball '95 in Columbus, Georgia.

O'Brien's Olympic debut against Puerto Rico was a productive one as she delivered singles in the USA's three-run third inning and again in a five-run sixth to help lead her team to a 10-0 rout of Puerto Rico. O'Brien completed the event with a .300 batting average with three hits, scored once and was perfect in the field at 1.000.

O'Brien's dimpled, All-American good looks give testimony that female athletes can be both athletic and feminine. To illustrate the point, O'Brien delivered a triple during the 1995 NCAA National Championship. After rounding the bases at full gait, O'Brien slid into third head first in time to beat the tag. Seemingly unimpressed with herself,

Photos on these pages courtesy of USA Softball/Doug Hoke

career at the University of Arizona where she was an important component of the NCAA National Championship teams in 1993 and 1994 and the runner-up team of 1995. In 1994, she batted .416 and was a unanimous NCAA first-team selection, a member of the All-Pacific Region and All-Pac 10 as well as a first-team Academic All-American. In 1995, O'Brien batted .433 with 21 doubles, three triples, two home runs and 62 RBI. She capped off the season with her second first-team NCAA All-America selection. She will again compete for Arizona in her senior season in 1997.

she casually dusted off her uniform, checked her nails and then prepared to go home on the next opportunity.

O'Brien began blossoming as a player at Don Antonio Lugo High School in Chino, CA., O'Brien was named Conference Most Valuable Player, All-League, first-team All-CIF, All-San Bernadino County, Inland Valley MVP -- three times each -- and CIF Player of the Year in 1990.

Her Olympic selection interrupted her college

DOT RICHARDSON

Dot Richardson's journey to the Olympics has been a long one, spanning almost two decades. Richardson has shared eight gold medals with her teammates since her debut in 1979, including three in the Pan American Games, two in the World Championships and one at the 1996 Olympic Games.

Ironically, Richardson's playing career began on the baseball field where at age eight she routinely tossed the ball around with her brother and father, occasionally serving as a bat girl and waiting patiently for her moment to take her position between the chalk lines.

A jarring experience on the ballfields of Orlando, Florida at age 10 forever altered her life and set in motion a chain of events that would ultimately lead to her present status as perhaps the best shortstop to have ever played the game.

"My brother and I were throwing the ball around when a man came over and asked if I would like to play on his little league team. I can't tell you how excited I was, because this was

Photos on this page courtesy of USA Softball/Doug Hoke

my dream, finally someone understood me. Finally, someone was going to give me a chance to play," Richardson said.

Richardson went from hyperspace to ground zero on the stranger's next words. "We'll cut your hair short and give you a boy's name," he said.

Richardson was devastated. For the first time, she became painfully aware that she was being passed over not because she couldn't play, but because she was a girl.

"If they told me I couldn't play because I wasn't fast enough, I could have understood it. But, being told I couldn't play because I was a girl, that was tough. That was something I could not control," Richardson said.

Later that afternoon, Richardson and a friend were back on the ballfields of Downey Park in Orlando. "We found an out of the way spot on the far end of the fields so that we would not interfere with the players. Suddenly, I looked up to see a man walking toward us. 'Coach Perkins would like to speak with you. Follow me,' he said."

"My first thoughts? Here we go again. But, I followed," she said.

Richardson's destination was a third base dugout. From the shadows she could hear a woman's voice asking her, "Have you ever played softball?"

"What's that," Richardson replied.

The coach handed her a ball and told her to get on third. Moments later, Richardson was tossing the ball around and thinking to herself, "This is not a major adjustment, I can do this."

Five minutes later, even though she had not recognized it at the time, Richardson had completed a mini-tryout and earned herself a position on Carol Perkins' Union Park Jets women's class A team.

The gender issue resolved, Richardson was now faced with the hurdle of playing on a team in which the average player was twice her age. Richardson's parents permitted her to play and

page one of the Richardson legend was about to be written. By season's end, Richardson had not only earned herself a starting position at third, but was named to the league all-star team.

A couple of seasons later at age 13, Richardson earned a spot on the Orlando Rebels, making her the youngest to ever play on a women's major team (photo below).

In college, she led UCLA in hitting three consecutive years, 1981-1983, was named to four NCAA All-American teams and was recognized as the NCAA Player of the Decade for the 80's.

In national play, Dot has been named to countless ASA All-American teams and is a seven-time Erv Lind Award winner, recognizing her as the best defensive player in the ASA Women's Major National Championship.

Richardson won her first USA gold medal in 1979 at the Pan American Games in San Juan, Puerto Rico. She followed with a silver in 1983 and another gold in the 1995 Pan American Games in Argentina. In Argentina, Richardson batted .469 with 15 hits and 10 RBI and was errorless in the field.

In World Championship play, she has been perfect,

Photo courtesy of National Softball Hall of Fame

Life can deal you very tough cards. Friend help your hand out.

knocking down gold medals in 1986 in New Zealand and 1994 in Canada. She has also picked up USA gold at the 1994 South Pacific Classic in Australia and at Superball '95 in Columbus, Georgia.

When someone tells Richardson she has the best hands in the game it rings with double meaning. Recognized as perhaps the best shortstop to have ever played the game, Richardson's hands are sure and precise but never more so than in life away from the field as an orthopedic surgeon.

During the grueling ordeal of attempting to make softball's first Olympic team, Richardson had the grit to also attempt to make it in one of the world's most demanding professions. As a medical student at the University of Louisville, Richardson's schedule was full, but somehow she managed to squeeze in her

first love of softball wherever she could, even if it included flying to Connecticut each week-end to play ball for her team, the Raybestos Brakettes.

Each Friday afternoon, Richardson would leave a medical staff meeting at 5 p.m. to catch a 5:30 p.m. flight to La Guardia Airport, changing from her scrubs into her uniform on the plane. From there it was a limo to the field for doubleheaders Friday, Saturday and Sunday and then back to Louisville to resume her rounds on Monday.

Once the decision to include softball in Atlanta was firm, Richardson made her commitment to pursue her Olympic dream as well as begin a five-year orthopedic surgery residency at the University of Southern California.

Photos on these pages courtesy of USA Softball/Doug Hoke

"I found myself at a crossroads between the career of my dreams in medicine and an Olympic dream I had held on to since I was ten years old. I decided to try to do both."

How many people told Richardson she was crazy and that there wasn't a future in softball, that she couldn't and shouldn't try to juggle the sport and her medical studies?

"I've heard it all my life, it's nice now to be able to say I made the right choice," Richardson said.

The choice did in fact turn out to be the right one for Richardson as she became the embodiment of the Olympics for millions. Her gleeful exuberance and demonstrated grasp of the moment made her softball's Olympic icon.

Richardson's Olympic debut was scripted in her dreams. She had publicly stated that her dream was to hit a home run in her first at-bat in Olympic competition and then later to deliver the game winning home run for the gold medal. Richardson would have to settle for the first USA hit of the Olympics as leadoff batter for the team. The home run didn't come until the sixth inning. Richardson also contributed a home run in game two against the Netherlands, this time scoring teammates Dionna Harris and Shelly Stokes.

In the final against China, Richardson fulfilled the remainder of her dream with a two-RBI home run in the third inning that also scored teammate Laura Berg. The triumphant trek around the bases that followed remains an indelible memory in the minds of everyone who witnessed it. Richardson finished the competition with a team leading 33 at-bats and 20 total bases and three home runs (tied) and was second in hits (9); runs (7); doubles (2); home runs (3) and RBI (7).

"There would be no Dot Richardson, Olympian, if the great players in the past had not taken the time to help a 10-year old kid learn the game. I have had the great privilege to learn from the best. The Olympics was a special moment that was shared with everyone who helped make it possible," she said.

JULIE SMITH

Julie Smith has been a standard bearer for the sport of softball since her USA Softball debut at the 1987 ISF Jr. Girls' World Championship in Oklahoma City.

And what a standard that has been, six international events -- six gold medals, including one in the sport's Olympic debut in 1996.

Smith earned her Olympic medal with play that included an impressive game three performance that featured three hits in three at-bats and two runs.

Smith started the USA off in the bottom of the first inning against Japan with a single to center. Teammate Lisa Fernandez's follow-up single advanced Smith to second just in time for Kim Maher's bases-clearing home run that put the USA up 3-0.

Smith singled again in the second and the sixth inning. In the sixth, Smith became a part of another big three-run inning for the USA. The USA's Laura Berg was on when Smith delivered a single to rightfield. It was déjà vu for Smith as a home run, this time delivered by Lisa Fernandez, again cleared the bases.

Home runs by Maher and Fernandez and a three-hit, two-run performance by Smith gave Japan their first loss of the Olympics (6-1).

Smith completed her Olympic debut batting .238 with five hits, two runs, an RBI and a perfect defensive performance (1.000).

A product of the ASA Junior Olympic youth program, Smith

in hitting (.359), single season at-bats (263) and runs scored (100) and led Fresno State in hitting in 1991 (.362).

Nationally, Smith has been equally successful as an ASA All-American selection and a recipient of the coveted Erv Lind Award denoting her as the top defensive player at the 1993 Women's Major National Championship. She was also a member of the Redding Rebels national championship teams of 1993, 1994 and 1995. She also has a fourth national title as a member of the 1987 Orange County Majestics of Orange County, California.

Internationally, Smith has been perfect, helping the USA establish its dominance in world play in the last decade. Besides her gold at the Jr. World's in 1987, Smith has also put the champion medal around her neck at the 1991 Pan American Games in Cuba, the 1994 ISF World Championships in Canada, the 1994 South Pacific Classic in Australia and the 1995 Pan American Games in Argentina.

MICHELE SMITH

On July 21, 1986, Michele Smith was thrown from an car, severing the muscle and nerve endings in her golden pitching arm. The accident forced her to not only face the trauma of her injury, but also the apparent end of her life as she had known it.

"For the first time I realized that my total persona revolved around my life as a pitching star. It appeared that my life as

has triumphed at every level of play, first at the juniors with her 1987 Jr. World title and then into college play where she led a talented Fresno State University team through its glory days of the early '90's. In the process, Julie was named to the NCAA's first team All-American squad in 1990-1991, recognized as one of the impact players of the '90's by her selection to the NCAA's Women's College World Series All-Decade team in 1991 and Fresno State's Athlete of the Year in 1990-91.

During her career at Fresno State, Smith posted team records

Photos on these pages courtesy of USA Softball/Doug Hoke

a pitcher and as Michele Smith was over," she said.

Michele's life was far from over, though, and after nine intensive months of rehabilitation she made her softball comeback as a pitcher at Oklahoma State University. She completed her college career as a two-time NCAA All-American.

In the years following, Smith has become a national and international sports superstar. In 1991, 1993, 1994 and 1995 she was named the Most Valuable Pitcher of the ASA Women's Major National Championship leading her team, the Redding Rebels of Redding, California to three consecutive national championships.

In college, Smith compiled an 82-20 pitching record with 46 shutouts and an .804 winning percentage at Oklahoma State University and batted .393 and .379 in her junior and senior seasons. She has also been named to numerous ASA All-American Teams as well as being honored as the United States Olympic Committee's Sportswoman of the Year for softball in 1990, 1993 and 1994.

In international play, Smith has led the USA to gold medals

at the 1993 Women's Challenger Cup in Beijing, China; the 1993 Intercontinental Cup in Holland; the 1994 South Pacific Classic in Australia and the 1994 ISF World Championship in Canada. She has never lost a game representing the USA.

In 1995, Smith led the USA to their third consecutive Pan American Games gold medal, pitching a 4-0 shutout against Puerto Rico in the final. During the event she also posted a .429 batting average and a team-leading three home runs.

Michele is well traveled internationally and is fluent in Japanese and in 1994 was named

MVP of the Japan League. She is also widely recognized as one of the sport's great ambassadors and has offered her considerable talents as a speaker, teacher and motivator to numerous charitable causes.

In one of life's ironic twists, Smith found herself on the field when the sport debuted in its first Olympics exactly ten years to the day, July 21, 1996, after what appeared to be her career ending accident.

"In 1986 I was faced with the reality that I might never pitch again. Sometimes it's hard for me to believe that after all that has happened, my Olympic dream actually came true," Smith said.

Smith's performance in the Olympics featured a dual role as pitcher and designated hitter. In game one against Puerto Rico, Smith produced a hit, a run and scored teammate Lisa Fernandez when she walked with the bases loaded in the first inning.

In game two against the Netherlands, Smith added another hit, run and RBI when she singled to score Sheila Cornell in the second inning. Smith also scored on a single to center by Dionna Harris.

Smith's first start in the circle came in game three against Japan in which she quickly retired the first seven batters before surrendering a hit and a walk in the third inning. Smith regrouped in the fourth sending three straight batters, two on strikeouts, back to the dugout.

Japan scored their lone run on Smith and the USA in the top of the fifth when leadoff hitter Haruka Saito put a pitch into the right field bleachers. The USA had already scored three in the first and later three more in the sixth to give Smith the 6-1 win.

Smith's final start of the Olympics came in game seven against China. After a shaky start in the first inning that included a single, a hit batter and two passed balls, Smith settled down, closed out the inning, and escaped unscathed.

She followed by retiring the next 12 batters in a row, taking the USA into the top of the sixth with a slim 1-0 lead even though they had outhit the Chinese 6-1 to that point. China took advantage of the USA's inability to convert runs and mounted a serious challenge in the sixth that include a two-RBI home run to put them into the lead at 2-1.

The USA responded in the bottom of the inning with a two-run blast of their own off the bat of Sheila Cornell that scored Kim Maher who had reached on a walk. Smith went three up/three down in the seventh to secure the critical win.

Smith remembers softball's debut in the Olympics as a beginning and not a destination. "When I walked onto the field the first time it was like walking

through a doorway from what had been to what will be for the future. I'm glad I could be a part of what the sport has achieved so far and hopefully a part of its new dreams for the future."

SHELLY STOKES

In 1995, Shelly Stokes made her USA Softball debut in the Pan American Games in Argentina batting .308 with four hits, scoring four times and producing a perfect defensive performance behind the plate.

Stokes has been involved in sports since her early days and began playing softball at age eight. Even at an early age, she was already dreaming about someday being an Olympic athlete.

In 1992, Stokes scuttled her Olympic dream to pursue a career in health care. It was a tough decision to closet her catcher's gear as she turned to soothing the pains and strains of her patients as a recreational therapist. However, even though the dream had faded it had not vanished. Encouraged by the

During her collegiate career, Shelly established herself as one of the best defensive catchers in the game at Fresno State University, going errorless in 386 total chances in 1989. She played in her share of big games at Fresno State and made four appearances (1987, 1988, 1989, 1990) at the NCAA Women's College World Series.

In 238 games at Fresno State, Stokes accumulated 174 hits in 695 at-bats, scored 79 runs and 68 RBI. In 1989, she also led the team in triples and was named a NCAA All-American in 1990.

Stokes began her international preparation at the 1995 Pan American Games in Argentina where she took her first of two USA gold medals that year. The second medal came at Superball '95 in Columbus, Georgia.

long-awaited announcement that softball would in fact be an Olympic sport in 1996, Stokes dug out the old mitt and aluminum bat and headed back to the softball field to rekindle her hope of being among the first chosen as softball Olympians.

"Traveling and competing in softball can be a challenge to your finances and career. I didn't think there was anything else for me to prove in softball so I figured it was time to move on. Then I heard the Olympic announcement and decided I wanted to be ready if I had the opportunity to be a part of the team," she said.

Getting ready meant a change of lifestyle for Stokes as she worked toward regaining the performance level she had attained in college.

Stokes went on to win a third USA gold medal in the Olympic Games when she teamed with pitchers Christa Williams, Lori Harrigan and Lisa Fernandez for wins against the Netherlands (9-0) and Chinese Taipei (4-0) before suffering a tough 2-1 loss to Australia.

Stokes had her shining Olympic moment at bat in game four against Chinese Taipei when she sacrificed Michele Smith home to give the USA a 2-0 lead.

DANI TYLER

Dani Tyler, without a doubt, owns one of the most infamous moments in the Olympics. But it was her handling of the moment that endeared her to thousands around the country.

In game six against Australia, Tyler became an instant, if not stunned, hero for the thousands of fans who had squeezed into Golden Park in Columbus, Georgia to witness a billed battle between two of the titans of international softball.

With two outs and Australian pitcher Tanya Harding bearing down on every delivery, Tyler did the seemingly impossible by delivering a gargantuan blow that reached the seventh row of the centerfield bleachers. She had done it, she had delivered a home run in the Olympic Games.

But, wait a minute, roll back the tape. In Tyler's exuberant celebration at home plate with teammate Laura Berg, she had done the unthinkable. Could she have forgotten to step on home plate, really?

The home plate umpire had missed the gaffe completely. Australia had not. On appeal, Tyler was credited with a triple and then called out at the plate, and the run and Tyler's shining Olympic moment were erased. Salt to the wound, the Australians stunned the USA in the bottom of the tenth with a home run of their own to complete the 2-1 upset in the strangest, yet perhaps the most riveting game in international softball history.

But what toll had it taken on youthful Olympian Tyler? Tyler's handling of the matter made her a hero.

Instead of blaming teammates, throwing her bat or refusing to talk about the incident, Tyler sucked it up and before a packed press conference admitted she had simply made a mistake. "I was very excited. I just can't believe I missed it. But it was my mistake. I should have made a better effort to look right at it and step right on it. From now on, I'll probably put a big 'X marks the spot' and step on it with both feet."

Even in Tyler's youth she demonstrated great wisdom by not allowing the incident to be a ball and chain that she would have to drag around for life. "I have to admit that it was a little hard to get out of bed the next morning, but one play doesn't make a game and I won't let one play define my life," she said.

Peter King, a writer for *Sports Illustrated* was among those in attendance at the event along with his 10-year old daughter Mary Beth. According to King, Mary Beth, a budding softballer of her own, had formed an immediate bond with Tyler when she noticed she was wearing her number 12 on her jersey. Mary Beth, according to her dad, was feeling a little down after the incident, not because of the lost run, but because she thought Tyler might be feeling bad about it.

Photos on these pages courtesy of USA Softball/Doug Hoke

Takes a better person to admitt to her Mistakes, nationally.

Truely, one play does not make or break a game.

A Follower of a hero.

After the game, King took a moment and related the story to Tyler. Tyler responded by asking him to wait while she made a dash to the team van to retrieve her wristbands and batting glove that had already been stowed. "Give these to Mary Beth," she said. "Tell her I'm sorry I let her down."

Tyler received a loud ovation from the fans when she entered the lineup for the next game against China, proof positive that Tyler had let no one down, except maybe herself. Tyler completed the Olympics with three hits, a run, a double, a triple (home run) and as expected, was perfect defensively.

Dani Tyler's golden glove and classic fielding style have made her a favorite of softball coaches everywhere. Her attitude toward the game also makes her among the sport's most coachable athletes. "I've never been the best athlete, but I try to have the best attitude and work the hardest," she said.

Tyler's Olympic odyssey began in 1993 when she applied for a spot at one of the Amateur Softball Association's Olympic tryout camps. She progressed through the levels and the evaluators liked what they saw and invited her to play on the 1994 Pan American Games Qualifier team. In her international debut, Tyler batted .257 with nine hits, five RBI and scored five times. As expected, she was superb defensively.

In 1995, Tyler competed at the

U.S. Olympic Festival in Denver, CO, where her west team won the bronze medal. "At the Festival, I was competing against the best players in the world," she said. "Any of the girls there could have made the team. I was just fortunate enough to be named."

Tyler began her preparations at Drake University where she batted .395 in her first three seasons. She was named the Missouri Valley Conference Rookie of the Year in 1993 and to the All-Conference team.

In 1994, she led the team in eight offensive categories including hitting (.384), slugging percentage (.647), at-bats (190), hits (73), RBI (50), doubles (16) and home runs (9).

In 1995, Tyler was at the top of her game, batting .462 with 11 doubles and 37 RBI and was once again named to the first-team All-Missouri Valley Conference and All-Midwest Region team.

The biggest award, however, came on September 4, 1995, when she was named to the first-ever Olympic softball team. "Making the team is a dream come true for me. Now that I've finally made it, I want to represent the USA to the best of my ability," she said.

America was proud of Dani Tyler in 1996.

CHRISTA WILLIAMS

In 1994, Christa Williams was making headlines in her hometown as she dominated the world of 5-A high school softball in Houston, Texas. As the ace of the Dobie High School softball team, Williams' reputation in her home state was soaring. Big things began to happen for Christa.

"I received a letter from USA Softball notifying me that my application to try out for the Olympic Team had been accepted. I was shocked and excited at the same time. I didn't even know I had applied," she said.

It turns out that her mentor (and dad) Ed Williams, sent in the application without telling her.

Williams impressed the evaluators and at the age of 16 became the youngest player to be invited to the 1994 USA Softball Women's National Team Camp.

At the camp, Williams proved that the "stuff" which worked so well against her high school chums was also effective against some of the USA's top hitters. Her performance earned a spot on the 1995 Pan Am Qualifier Team that won a gold medal in Guatemala.

If Williams was nervous about her international debut, it didn't show. In her first outing against El Salvador, she pitched a no-hitter and followed four games later with a one-hitter against Belize. Williams' 15-0 perfect-game performance against Nicaragua launched her into the

national and international spotlight. Williams ended her Guatemala debut with a 0.00 ERA, three shutouts and 45 strikeouts.

The successes of 1994 were only a prologue to Williams' 1995 performance that included a 6-0 gold medal run at the ISF Junior World Championships in July. Williams led arguably the best USA Junior World team ever to a 15-0 rout of an impressive, 14-nation field. Her personal stats included a perfect 6-0 record, a 0.00 ERA and a tournament leading 86 strikeouts.

At age 18, Williams was the resident rookie on a team filled with softball legends. Her performance in the Games proved that she belonged.

Williams appeared tentative in her first debut innings in the Olympics, allowing the Netherlands to mount a challenge

in the second inning with a pair of hits. However, the USA bats were smoking in the bottom of the second, producing five runs on six hits to give Williams a 5-0 cushion.

Williams' youthful butterflies fluttered away as she retired 15 of the next 16 batters she faced, eight on strikes, to lead the USA to a 9-0 rout of the Netherlands. In game five, the USA found themselves in a tough battle with Canada. USA Starter Michele Granger had issued a pair of

Photo at top of page courtesy of USA Softball
Remainder of photos on these pages courtesy of USA Softball/Doug Hoke

to the drama by loading the bases on a fielding error on her first batter. Williams went after the next two batters, retiring the first on strikes and the second on a pop up to left field.

Williams' retired the side in the sixth and the USA scored a pair of runs in the seventh to take a 4-2 lead into the bottom of the inning. Two strikeouts and a dramatic pick-off at second base closed out the inning and gave Williams her second win of the Olympics.

Williams completed the event with a pair of wins, 15 strikeouts and a perfect 0.00 ERA. The rookie had earned the right to call herself an Olympic champion.

asked to consider coaching his first women's softball team. Raymond was not sure that he was interested; after all his schedule was pretty full coaching American legion baseball, high school football and a couple of men's major fast pitch softball clubs in his hometown of Worcester, Mass.

walks and hits during the first four innings of the contest. The USA's Dot Richardson scored in the fourth on a single, a sacrifice by Julie Smith and a throwing error to give the USA a precarious 1-0 lead. They scored again in the top of the fifth to lead 2-0.

Canada jumped on Granger in the bottom of the fifth to produce a pair of singles, a triple, a walk and two runs to knot the game at 2-2.

With two on, one out and the game on the line, the USA's teen phenom was in the pressure cooker as she was brought in to relieve Granger. Williams added

HEAD COACH RALPH RAYMOND

In 1996, Ralph Raymond reached the mountain top of his career as the most prolific coach in USA Softball history by taking the USA team to the gold medal at the sport's Olympic debut.

Raymond's softball career has covered a lot of ground, beginning in 1963 when he was

Raymond was already somewhat of a sports legend in the city, having captained his high school baseball, football and basketball teams before passing on a promising professional baseball career to pursue his first love of teaching.

Even so, Raymond was still open to the idea, which led to a meeting with the sponsor of a women's major club from Cochituate, Massachusetts. "When I left for the meeting I wasn't sure I wanted to do that. But I went down to Cochituate and stayed there four years."

From the start, Raymond demonstrated a propensity for

winning the big ones. In 1965, his team, Cochituate Motors, was invited to participate in an annual July softball tournament in Stratford, Connecticut, home of the renown Raybestos Brakettes. "So we went down and we beat them (the Brakettes)," Raymond said.

The Brakettes were so dominant in women's fast pitch and so highly favored that tournament organizers had already engraved their names on the winner plaques. "We had to wait around until midnight to get the plaques changed to read Cochituate Motors," Raymond chuckled.

The win proved to be an important one for Raymond as it resulted in a phone call the following day from William S. Simpson, Chairman of the Board and President of Raybestos. Raymond was on his way to Stratford as an assistant to manager Vin DeVitt.

Two years later, after DeVitt's retirement, Raymond took over the Brakettes and over the next three decades established them as one of the all-time great and enduring sport dynasties, amassing an incredible 18 national titles and seven runner-up finishes.

Raymond's career record of 1,992 wins and only 162 losses with the Brakettes is second to none.

In 1994, Raymond wrote the final chapter on his Brakette saga and turned the page that led him

into perhaps his greatest challenge ever as softball's first-ever Olympic coach.

"We carried the torch for the Joanie Joyces, the Bertha Tickeys, the Barbie Reinaldas, the Kathy Arendsens and all the others who put in their time, hoping some day they'd be able to play in the Olympics. We were torch bearers for the young ladies in the past and future," he said.

Raymond's international record is imposing. As head coach of the USA Softball Women's National Teams, he has produced four gold medals in ISF World Championship play, including three consecutive (1986, 1990, 1994) for a combined record of 63-0.

He has also produced 12 other gold medals representing the USA in competitions including the Pan American Games (1967, 1979, 1995); World Games (1981, 1985); Intercontinental Cup (1985, 1993); World Cup (1986); Challenger Cup (1992); South Pacific Classic (1994); and Superball '95 (1995).

"Being named softball's first Olympic coach was a pinnacle point in my career. Winning the gold medal meant that I've finally reached the top of the mountain," he said.

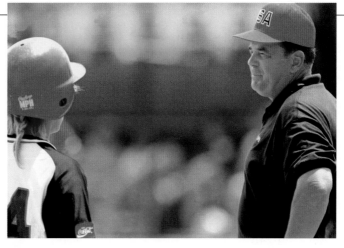

ASSISTANT COACH RALPH WEEKLY

Ralph Weekly, assistant coach of the USA Softball women's gold medal team, is considered among the finest hitting clinicians in the nation.

1990. He was also named the NAIA National Coach of the Year in 1986, 1987, 1988, 1989, 1990, 1992, 1993 and 1994.

After an eight-year tenure at Pacific, Weekly moved to the University of Tennessee-Chattanooga in 1995 and in his first season went 29-19 and tied for the regular season conference championship. During his collegiate career he has compiled a record of 350-118 (.748).

Internationally, Weekly served as head coach of the USA team that went 15-0 to win the gold medal at the 1995 Pan American Games Qualifier in Guatemala. In 1995, he also served as an assistant coach of the USA team that won their third consecutive gold medal in the 1995 Pan American Games in Argentina.

Before beginning his collegiate coaching career, Weekly served in the U.S. Air Force from 1960-86 and was commander of the Air Force Office of Special Investigations at McChord AFB in Washington. During his military career he coached three Armed Forces Worldwide Champions.

Weekly has been in the college coaching ranks since 1986 when he took his first job at Pacific Lutheran University. While at Pacific, Weekly won NAIA national titles in 1988 and 1992 and finished as the runner-up in

ASSISTANT COACH MARGIE WRIGHT

Margie Wright has spent almost two decades amassing one of the best national and international coaching records in the sport of softball.

After serving six seasons at Illinois State, where she compiled a record of 614-225-3 (.729), Margie was hired as the head coach of the Fresno State Bulldogs. Through the 1996 season, Wright has compiled a record of 566-175-1 (.764) at Fresno State, making her the winningest coach in FSU history. Her teams have advanced to the NCAA regionals 11 straight years and to the NCAA Women's College World Series in seven of the last ten.

She is ranked among the leaders in wins (715) and winning percentage (.736) among NCAA Division I coaches. She is also only the fourth coach in NCAA Division I history to record more than 700 career wins.

Wright has also served as a coach for numerous USA Softball national teams and as an ambassador for the sport of softball. In 1989, she became the first softball coach to travel to a communist country as a clinician. She also represented the U.S. Information Agency (USIA) in Czechoslovakia where she conducted clinics in several cities for a variety of teams.

In 1994, Wright helped coach the USA Softball Women's National Team to their third consecutive gold medal at the ISF Women's World Championship in St. John's, Newfoundland, Canada. In 1995, she also served as the head coach of the USA Softball Junior Women's National Team that won the 1995 ISF Junior Women's World Championship in Normal, Illinois and as an assistant coach for the gold medal-winning USA Softball Women's National Team at Superball '95 in Columbus, Georgia.

Photos on this page courtesy of USA Softball/Doug Hoke

TEAM LEADER RONNIE ISHAM

In many respects, the long, tall Texan from Stephenville was the glue that held the USA Softball Women's National Team together through its extensive national team tour and run to the gold in the 1996 Olympic Games.

Among his many roles, Isham also served as a member of the National Team Selection Committee.

Isham has extensive experience in his position as team leader including participation at the 1993 Junior Men's World Championship in Auckland, New Zealand; 1994 South Pacific Classic in Sidney, Australia; 1995 USA Softball Olympic Tour in Australia; 1995 Pan American Games in Parana, Argentina; the 1996 Coca-Cola USA Softball National Team Tour; and the 1996 Centennial Olympic Games in Columbus, Georgia.

He has also held numerous positions within the Amateur Softball Association and was recently named commissioner of one of the ASA's largest state associations in Texas.

Isham's position as team leader required him to be the on-site diplomat and general "work it out" point man in issues involving players, coaches, association officials and numerous other entities. Isham, above all, was responsible for keeping the wheels of the Olympic train well oiled and moving down the track toward its destination.

His positions on the National Selection Committee and as Team Leader required extreme personal sacrifices in the years leading up to the selection of the Olympic Team and the year following. Whenever there was a job that had to be done, Isham was always on target to work it through completion, resulting in a gold medal for the USA at the 1996 Olympic Games.

6

PREPARING
FOR
DESTINY'S
CALL

LEFT: *The Olympic torch passes through Oklahoma City.*

INSET: *Dionna Harris and the Olympic Flame.*
Photos courtesy of USA Softball/Doug Hoke

After the announcement of the Olympic team on September 4, 1995, there was a new focus for USA Softball. No longer was the job to find the right players; after almost three years of exhaustive work that task had been accomplished. The new goal, the target that had mattered the most all along, was to win the gold medal.

The players had never been involved in a selection process like the one they had just completed. It was a process that had altered everyone's life and put a lot of decision-making and future plans on hold. For those who were passed over, their lives could be reclaimed and they were enabled to move forward with other commitments and goals. For those who were chosen, the real commitment to themselves, their team and their country had only begun.

Following a number of organizational meetings including a team unity camp at the U.S. Olympic Committee's training center in Colorado Springs, the team finally began to shake off the months of competition that had been completed and wake up to their new role as Olympians.

The action began in earnest when the USA was invited to tour Australia in November of 1995. It was an expensive and ambitious undertaking for the program, especially since the team had hardly practiced together since their selection only two months earlier. It was also an opportunity that

USA Softball officials and coaches knew they could not let pass by. From a preparation standpoint, it provided competition against one of the top international programs via Olympic medal contender Australia. USA Softball officials also fully understood the importance of thinking past 1996. Softball was on the program for now, but there were no guarantees for the 2000 Olympic Games in Sydney.

. . . .

THIS PAGE: *Australia Tour.*
Photo courtesy of USA Softball

OPPOSITE PAGE: *At press conference announcing the 1996 USA Olympic Softball Team, the countdown to the gold had begun.*
Photo courtesy of USA Softball/Doug Hoke

create interest in the sport, support that softball would need if it was to continue on the program.

Australia proved to be a great host even if the USA was less than gracious in their visits to Sydney, New South Wales, Canberra and Brisbane. If there were any doubts that the USA was the team to beat in the Olympics, they were quickly extinguished after the Americans returned after winning 13 straight games. Although many of the games featured local club teams, the tour also featured the Australia National Team. The time in Australia set a positive tone for the months of training that were yet to come.

It was critical that Sydney understood that the USA was in full support of their efforts to include softball on the program. A head-to-head Australia versus USA tour could only

. . . .

THIS PAGE: *Michele Smith in Australia.*

OPPOSITE PAGE (TOP LEFT): *Autograph session - Australia Tour.*

OPPOSITE PAGE (TOP RIGHT): *Christa Williams pitching in exhibition during Australia Tour.*

OPPOSITE PAGE (BOTTOM): *USA Softball Olympic Team (Australia Tour).*
Photos on these pages courtesy of USA Softball

For the next few months, the players scattered across the country as they attempted to organize, visualize and prepare for the training that began in earnest in April. Many of the players conducted clinics or put their professional careers and personal lives on temporary hold.

Dot Richardson, a third-year resident in orthopedic surgery, prepared herself and her colleagues for a year-long sabbatical. Among the terms of Richardson's orthopedic release was her agreement to report back to full-time duty just two days after the completion of the Olympic competition. Three players, Laura Berg, Dani Tyler and Leah O'Brien, postponed the completion of their collegiate softball careers to make a run at the gold. Michele Granger and Martha O'Kelley prepared for difficult separations from their husbands. Sheila Cornell's courtship with her fiancé would also have to wait. For all the ladies of USA Softball, there was some unfinished business in their lives that would wait no longer.

As the players packed their bags and prepared for the months ahead, USA Softball officials were working around the clock to lock down the details for a soon to be announced National Team tour.

The team would first assemble in their new home in Columbus, Georgia in mid-April and then embark on the most ambitious tour ever to be attempted in the sport. In the four months leading up to the Olympic Games, the USA team would complete 61 games in 23 cities and in the process receive the warm embrace of thousands of adoring fans from coast to coast.

. . . .
OPPOSITE PAGE: *Dr. Dot in medical school.*
Photo courtesy of National Softball Hall of Fame.

USA Team

Batting Statistics USA SOFTBALL TOUR

18 Player(s)	BA	AB	R	H	2B	3B	HR	RBI	BB	SO	SB	CS	SH	SF	HP	SLG
Cornell, S.	.447	103	43	46	7	0	14	39	16	6	1	0	1	0	1	.922
Stokes, S.	.438	64	16	28	4	1	5	21	12	3	2	0	2	2	2	.766
Harris, D.	.436	110	42	48	6	2	3	22	6	6	7	0	0	3	2	.609
Richardson, D.	.433	97	31	42	8	1	2	15	13	5	0	1	1	1	2	.598
Fernandez, L.	.402	127	46	51	5	0	7	35	20	3	0	0	0	2	2	.606
Maher, K.	.393	168	53	66	11	1	9	58	10	13	1	0	1	2	4	.631
Tyler, D.	.385	96	30	37	7	0	4	30	5	7	0	0	9	1	0	.583
Berg, L.	.379	87	25	33	1	0	1	17	7	1	1	0	1	1	1	.425
Venturella, M.	.377	53	14	20	3	0	1	15	8	7	1	0	1	1	0	.491
O'Kelley, M.	.367	30	10	11	2	0	0	6	5	6	0	0	0	2	0	.433
Boxx, G.	.357	70	23	25	1	0	5	22	12	3	1	0	2	0	0	.586
Smith, J.	.348	92	28	32	2	1	1	11	4	1	5	0	5	0	2	.424
McFalls, J.	.330	88	25	29	2	0	3	25	8	10	1	0	0	1	0	.455
O'Brien, L.	.329	85	18	28	3	1	1	12	11	4	2	0	3	0	1	.424
Smith, M.	.326	89	24	29	5	1	2	24	14	11	0	0	1	1	0	.472
Jordan, B.	.308	52	16	16	1	0	0	7	13	2	1	1	0	0	1	.327
Brundage, J.	.273	22	4	6	0	0	1	6	6	2	0	0	0	0	1	.409

Less than 10 Plate Appearances

	BA	AB	R	H	2B	3B	HR	RBI	BB	SO	SB	CS	SH	SF	HP	SLG
Williams, C.	1.000	1	1	1	0	0	0	0	0	0	0	0	0	0	0	1.000
Totals	.382	1434	449	548	68	8	59	365	170	90	23	2	27	17	21	.564

USA Team

Pitching Statistics USA SOFTBALL TOUR

5 Player(s)	IP	R	ER	H	HR	BB	HB	SO	WP	CG	W	L	SV	ERA
Smith, M.	73.0	0	0	5	0	12	0	138	0	12	12	0	0	0.00
Fernandez, L.	70.0	0	0	2	0	2	2	179	0	13	14	0	0	0.00
Harrigan, L.	82.0	1	1	21	0	15	2	157	0	12	13	0	0	0.11
Granger, M.	67.0	1	1	5	0	6	2	169	1	12	11	1	0	0.13
Williams, C.	64.0	1	1	11	0	11	0	124	1	10	10	0	0	0.14
Totals	356.0	3	3	44	0	46	6	767	2	59	60	1	0	0.08

* The 60 - 1 record reflects 3 extra games that were not counted towards the final tour record. The official tour record is 57 - 1 (.982).

1996 Coca-Cola® USA Softball® Tour presented by IGA®
Schedule

Date	Site	Facility	Time	Attendance	Results			Overall Record
Friday, April 26	at Sacramento, CA	Sacramento Sports Complex	6:30/8:30 PM	3,000	USA 4 - Lynchmob	0		1 - 0
					USA 13 - Sac. City	0		2 - 0
Saturday, April 27	at Sacramento, CA	Sacramento Sports Complex	3:00/5:00 PM	3,000	USA 8 - Sac City	0		3 - 0
					USA 7 - Lynch Mob	0		4 - 0
Friday , May 3	at Los Angeles, CA	Mayfair Park, Lakewood	7:00/9:00 PM	3,000	USA 7 - Cal. Select	0		5 - 0
					USA 0 - Cal. Select	1		5 - 1
Saturday, May 4	at Los Angeles, CA	Mayfair Park, Lakewood	2:00/4:00 PM	3,000	USA 1 - Cal. Select	0		6 - 1
					USA 3 - Cal. Select	0		7 - 1
Friday May, 10	at Phoenix, AZ	Cave Creek Sports Complex	6:00/8:00 PM	2,000	USA 4 - Phoenix Sunbirds	0		8 - 1
					USA 9 - Phoenix Sunbirds	0		9 - 1
Saturday, May 11	at Phoenix, AZ	Cave Creek Sports Complex	1:00/3:00 PM	2,000	USA 2 - Phoenix Sunbirds	0		10 - 1
					USA 4 - Phoenix Sunbirds	0		11 - 1
Friday, May 17	at Tulsa, OK	Broken Arrow High School	6:00/8:00 PM	3,000	USA 6 - High School A/S	0		12 - 1
					USA 2 - Tulsa A/S	0		13 - 1
* Saturday, May 18	at Oklahoma City, OK	Hall of Fame Stadium	4:00 PM	4,000	USA 13 - UCO	0		14 - 1
* Sunday, May 19	at Oklahoma City, OK	Hall of Fame Stadium	12:30/3:00 PM	4,000	USA 23 - OCU	0		15 - 1
					USA 8 - OCU	0		16 - 1
Monday, May 20	at Waco, TX	Baylor University	6:00/8:00 PM	3,000	USA 16 - Waco A's	0		17 - 1
					USA 7 - Waco A's	0		18 - 1
Tuesday, May 21	at Houston, TX	Memorial Park	7:00/8:30 PM	5,000	USA 7 - IGA All Stars	0		19 - 1
					USA 8 - IGA All Stars	0		20 - 1
Wednesday, May 22	at Lake Jackson, TX	MacLean Park	6:30/8:30 PM	5,500	USA 12 - LJ All-Stars	0		21 - 1
					USA 8 - LJ All-Stars	0		22 - 1
Friday, May 24	at Midland, TX	Bill Williams Park	6:00/8:00 PM	5,500	USA 1 - Sun Birds	0		23 - 1
					USA 3 - Sun Birds	0		24 - 1
Saturday, May 25	at Ft. Worth, TX	Gateway Park	6:00/8:00 PM	6,500	USA 3 - Power	0		25 - 1
					USA 12 - Ranger JC	0		26 - 1
Sunday, May 26	at Ft. Worth, TX	Gateway Park	6:00/8:00 PM	6,500	USA 8 - Blue Thunder	0		27 - 1
					USA 22 - Ft. Worth A/S	0		28 - 1
Friday, May 31	at Rock Island, IL	Allen Campbell Complex	7:00/9:00 PM	3,000	USA 4 - RI All Stars	0		29 - 1
					USA 8 - RI All Stars	0		30 - 1
Saturday, June 1	at Schaumburg, IL	Schaumburg Village	3:00/5:00 PM	2,000	USA 8 - Illusions	0		31 - 1
					USA 8 - Schaumburg A/S	0		32 - 1
Friday, June 7	at Hazleton, PA	Drifton Complex	6:30/8:30 PM	3,000	USA 9 - Drifton A/S	0		33 - 1
					USA 1 - Topton VIP	0		34 - 1

Date	Site	Facility	Time	Attendance	Results			Overall Record
Saturday, June 8	at Hazleton, PA	Drifton Complex	6:30/8:30 PM	3,000	USA 9 - Drifton A/S	0		35 - 1
					USA 6 - Drifton A/S	0		36 - 1
Tuesday, June 11	at Chattanooga, TN	Warner Park	6:00/8:00 PM	3,000	USA 3 - TN A/S	0		37 - 1
					RAIN OUT *			*Rain Out
Friday, June 14	at Akron, OH	Firestone Stadium	6:00/8:00 PM	4,500	USA 3 - Thunder	0		38 - 1
					USA 10 - Akon A/S	0		39 - 1
Saturday, June 15	at Ashland, OH	Ashland City Park	6:00/8:00 PM	4,500	USA 6 - Ashland A/S	0		40 - 1
					USA 5 - Ashland A/S	0		41 - 1
Tuesday, June 18	at Peachtree City, GA	N/A	6:00/8:00 PM	3,000	USA 8 - College A/S	0		42 - 1
					USA 8 - High School A/S	0		43 - 1
Friday, June 21	at Worcester, MA	Worcester State College	6:00/8:00 PM	3,000	USA 8 - N. E. All Stars	0		44 - 1
					USA 9 - N. E. All Stars	0		45 - 1
Saturday, June 22	at Worcester, MA	Worcester State College	6:00/8:00 PM	3,000	USA 16 - N. E. All Stars	0		46 - 1
					USA 5 - N. E. All Stars	0		47 - 1
Thursday, June 27	at Bloomington, IL	O'Neil Park	6:40/8:15 PM	3,000	USA 11 - Lady Hearts	0		48 - 1
					USA 15 - Pekin Letts	0		49 - 1
Friday, June 28	at Normal, IL	Maxwell Park	6:40/8:15 PM	3,000	USA 8 - Lady Hearts	0		50 - 1
					USA 9 - Normal A/S	0		51 - 1
Saturday, June 29	at Decatur, IL	Borg Warner Complex	7:00/9:00 PM	7,500	USA 10 - Decatur Pride	0		52 - 1
					USA 8 - Decatur Breeze	0		53 - 1
Sunday, June 30	at St. Louis, MO	ABC Park	6:00/8:00 PM	3,500	USA 4 - College A/S	0		54 - 1
					USA 1 - St. Louis Classic	0		55 - 1
Thursday, July 4	at Atlanta, GA	Softball Country Club	6:00/8:00 PM	5,000	USA 2 - TN All Stars	0		56 - 1
					USA 9 - Atlanta A/S	0		57 - 1
					USA 449 to Opponents	3		57 - 1 (.982)

THESE PAGES: *The USA Softball touring bus.* Photo courtesy of USA Softball/Doug Hoke

The organization of what became the Coca-Cola USA Softball National Team Tour was ambitious and difficult. Ralph Raymond, the team's head coach, had made it clear that the team needed at least 50 games under its belt before stepping into Olympic competition; USA Softball learned quickly that the task of steering a USA team entourage through 23 cities would be staggering. Besides the obvious issues of providing food, lodging and transportation, there were other difficulties — such as providing security for twenty young ladies who were rapidly becoming more and more visible to the world.

As in the pre-Olympic years, it was the local organizations of the Amateur Softball Association that stepped up and provided the way. Twenty-two such organizations came forward and offered their facilities for the tour. Since a tour of this magnitude had never been attempted, there was some risk involved. What if they held the competition and no one came?

As the details of the tour were being finalized, the team prepared to make their

RIGHT: *Judy Favor, Columbus College Women's Fast Pitch Softball Coach; Karen Sanchelli, USA Softball National Team member; Caren Napolitano and Chera Owens, Columbus College Softball Team; Lori Harrigan, USA Softball National Team member; Jennifer Deason and Angel Brooks, Pheonix City Girls Softball League, all contributed to a softball demonstration during the groundbreaking ceremony, at Golden Park in Columbus, Ga.*
Photo courtesy of USA Softball

LEFT: *Columbus Mayor Frank K. Martin championed the Columbus Olympic movement in the early days and helped bring softball to his city.* Photo courtesy of USA Softball

move to Columbus, Georgia. The city of Columbus, Georgia was selected as the team's home for a number of reasons. The humidity and heat of a July Olympic competition in Georgia could pose stamina problems for the players, especially since most were not used to Southern climates. The opportunity to train in the exact location that the Games would be played was an advantage. But most importantly, locating in Columbus gave the team an opportunity to bond with the community and vice versa. Support from the fans could be an important plus for a hometown favorite. The combination of community support and climate was just too great to pass by.

USA Softball team leader Ronnie Isham became the team's mother hen in the early days, keeping a wary eye on his charges. The safety of the athletes always remained of primary important. Most concerns were unfounded as the people of Columbus were proof positive that Southern hospitality was more fact than fabrication.

In fact, the city was so serious about making the team feel welcome that few player requests went unanswered. In fact, the team had to be careful because to ask in Columbus was to receive, as attested to by head coach Ralph Raymond. In a interview shortly after the team's arrival, Raymond joked that all he needed was his recliner to really feel at home. The next day a recliner was delivered to his door.

The practice areas provided by the city at the South Commons Complex, located just a stone's throw from the Olympic Stadium, were among the best anywhere in the country. The fields and the adjacent park

with the team on its tour stops in Tulsa and Oklahoma City and then produced a quality 30-minute documentary on the team that was aired just prior to the Olympic Games.

On the print side, the USA team was befriended by the sports staff at the *Columbus Ledger-Enquirer*. For a sport in search of an identity, the team of Chuck Williams, Molly Blue, Guerry Clegg, Mark Rice and Timothy Rogers helped paint a picture of not only a championship team but of the individual players who became its heart and soul. These journalists came in search of a story and found themselves becoming a part of it.

areas were exceptional. The complex was the perfect illustration of a city and a group of park employees who were proud of their role in history.

The team had achieved celebrity status in Columbus after their first appearance at Superball '95. Every word, every expression were likely to appear in print or on the evening sports broadcast. Ironically, the local NBC affiliate (the network of the Olympic Games) had no sports or news team and carried no local programming. One local broadcaster, WTVM-9, and its aggressive sports team of Dave Platta and Robbie Watson, were all over this story from the outset. Platta even took time to travel

. . . .

ABOVE: *Columbus welcomes the world.*

OPPOSITE PAGE: *USA Team at Golden Park in Columbus, GA - start of their residence leading up to the Olympics.*
Photos on these pages courtesy of USA Softball

The team began their preparations for the tour with daily workouts at South Commons. It was here that a group of great individual athletes began their metamorphosis into a great team.

After the tour began, the weekly routine included a week-end of competition and then back to Columbus for daily workouts. This routine continued for eleven consecutive weeks until its final tour date July 4 in Atlanta.

ABOVE LEFT: *Entrance to Golden Park, Columbus.*

OPPOSITE PAGE: *Dionna Harris and Kim Maher signing autographs at press conference in Oklahoma City.*
Photos on these pages courtesy of USA Softball/Doug Hoke

The tour began in Sacramento, California at the Sacramento Sports Complex and, as anticipated, included lopsided wins against the Lynchmob, 4-0, 7-0; and Sac City, 13-0, 8-0. The stop gave the USA team its first glimpse of what might be expected of them in the days ahead. Sell-out crowds of over 3,000 attended all four sessions April 26 and 27.

Along with enormous fan interest also came big expectations. It was evident immediately that the fans in attendance were expecting more than a casual spectator-athlete relationship with this team. There would be no satisfying the fans' need to feel a part of this special Olympic moment. The USA team, however, made the attempt and remained at the stadium for over 1½ hours following the completion of the first night's doubleheader, signing anything and everything that was pushed in front of them.

The demand for autographs was so high at some stops that local organizers began handing out 500 free tickets to the signings in an attempt to control the size of the sessions. Even at that, the days and evenings were long for the team and coaches.

The fans freely gave their support, and the players reponded with the gift of themselves.

One of the more memorable moments of the tour occurred when the team produced their own music tape and proceeded to lead fans in their rendition of "Y-M-C-A". There was not a face without a smile after watching Martha O'Kelley jump aboard an autograph table to lead the team and the crowd. The performance would become a regular occurrence during the final moments of the autograph sessions during the tour.

The tour progressed to Los Angeles and Mayfair Park in Lakewood, California on May 3-4. After a 7-0 thrashing of the California Select in the 7 p.m. game, the USA lost its only contest of the tour, 1-0, in the late game at 9 p.m. Despite the lateness of the hour and the loss, the players remained until almost 1 a.m., signing autographs and talking with fans.

. . . .
RIGHT: *USA Team leading the crowd in Y-M-C-A.* Photo courtesy of USA Softball/Doug Hoke

The tour continued on to Phoenix and the Cave Creek Sports Complex; to Tulsa at Broken Arrow High School and to ASA Hall of Fame Stadium in Oklahoma City.

LEFT: *The fans turned out to witness a special Olympic moment in Oklahoma City.*

OPPOSITE PAGE (TOP): *Kathy Arendsen.*

OPPOSITE PAGE (BOTTOM): *Lisa Fernandez with Miss America, Shawntel Smith.*
Photos on theses pages courtesy of USA Softball/Doug Hoke

The visit to Oklahoma City on May 18-19 was an exciting one that included a special Olympic celebration with an official visit by the Olympic torch on the 23rd day of its journey to Atlanta. An appearance by Miss America, Shawntel Smith, and the induction of the 1996 class of the National Softball Hall of Fame, which included former World and Pan American Games Champion Kathy Arendsen, made the weekend even more significant.

The Olympic torch made its way to ASA Hall of Fame Stadium as part of the pre-game festivities of a doubleheader with the Oklahoma City University Chiefs, who had just returned after successfully winning their third consecutive NAIA National Championship. At exactly 12:51 p.m., Olympic

torchbearer Col. James R. "Bob" Willis entered the stadium along the right field warning track to the sound of Olympic fanfare. By the time Willis had reached the first base line, everyone in the stadium had spotted him and were on their feet in celebration. The torch continued with a salute to the crowd at home and then down the third base line to a waiting caldron that was ignited while the celebration continued.

The USA team reacted like most of the other people in the stadium by whipping out their pocket cameras in hopes of recording the moment.

"It didn't hit me until we were in Oklahoma for the torch run. When I saw 5,000 people standing and cheering when they ran the torch into the stadium, I broke down. I had tears streaming down my face. I realized what it was all about. It's not just about me, the team or softball, it's about the whole country. It's about the whole United States. There's nothing that can compare to it," said Lisa Fernandez.

Miss America Shawntel Smith carried the torch the previous day and was on hand to provide a solo rendition of the national anthem backed by a local chorus and dance ensemble team that provided additional color to the event.

The USA completed its stop in Oklahoma City with three more victories, one against the

BELOW: *Players with the Olympic flame in Oklahoma City.*

OPPOSITE PAGE: *USA Team forms a kickline on the sidelines.*

PREVIOUS PAGES (LEFT): *USA Team snaps photos of the lighting of the torch.*

PREVIOUS PAGES (RIGHT): *Miss America, Shawntel Smith, performs national anthem.*

Photos on these pages courtesy of USA Softball/Doug Hoke

University of Central Oklahoma, 13 -0; and two against NAIA National Champion Oklahoma City 23-0, 8-0. With a record of 16-1, the USA pointed their bus toward Texas.

During the week that followed, the USA notched twelve more games with visits to Waco, Houston, Lake Jackson, Midland and Ft. Worth.

The Texas swing of the tour put the team in front of more than 32,000 fans with overflow audiences at each site including over 6,500 each session in Ft. Worth.

Besides the games and autograph sessions, the team

also conducted numerous free clinics that were attended by hundreds of young Olympic hopefuls at each site. As Fernandez said, "I can remember being their age and going to games and wishing the players would just turn and look at me or wave or just acknowledge me somehow. I know how much this means to them."

ABOVE : *Meeting the competition in Oklahoma City.*

OPPOSITE PAGE (BACKGROUND): *Oklahoma City University Chiefs.*

OPPOSITE PAGE : *Safe/Safe*

Photos on the these pages courtesy of USA Softball/Doug Hoke

It was an important day for me. To stand in the box and face Michele Smith, I was proud of myself to just foul-off a ball. But what really hit home was the roar of the crowd chanting my name as I ran to my familiar position in center.

It was also important to the players who were chosen to play the dominant Olympic team. In Lake Jackson, the USA competed against its only high school all-star team. All-star pitcher Tamika Mack made the most of the opportunity by striking out USA lead-off batter Dot Richardson on three consecutive strikes for the first out of the game. "I'll remember the strikeout the most. I never expected to strike out anyone."

April Williamson will remember stepping into the batter's box in her team's first at-bat against Michele Smith and producing a foul tip off the first pitch. "It was really, really scary. I wanted someone else to go first and strike out before me. Then I just wanted to foul it. When I did, it meant a lot. It's exciting."

But not too exciting. Smith struck out 13 of 15 batters she faced and the USA won the game 12-0 in five innings. "I've faced speed like that before, but nothing that moved like that. You look back and the catcher's mitt was a foot above you. We were all getting suckered by her riseball," said Erin Runci, a high school senior from Columbia, Texas.

It wasn't a matter of beating the USA, no one expected that. It was a matter of producing a foul tip, a strikeout and losing by twelve runs and still feeling good about it, like something other than winning was important.

The tour gave the next generation of Olympic hopefuls the opportunity to not only meet but to compete against the best in the world and perhaps to set their own sights on the gold in the years ahead. "I remember coming out to Lake Jackson for a clinic years ago and there were tons of kids here wanting to learn how to play the game. At that time, fast pitch softball wasn't even in high school. The reception that we received here was proof that the time was not wasted," said Michele Granger.

From Texas the tour turned East with stops in the Chicago area in Rock Island and Schaumburg and then to the Drifton Complex in Hazelton, Pennsylvania. The response in the East mirrored that of the West Coast and Texas with standing-room-only crowds for each contest.

For many the tour represented the Olympics. "The team's appearance was one of the greatest things that ever happened in this area. This was a once in a lifetime opportunity," said softball coach Pat Lausterer of Barnesville, Illinois.

"It was a great opportunity for the people who can't get to Atlanta to see the Olympics. It puts Hazelton on the map. I've had calls from the whole East Coast, they all wanted to come to Drifton. It was terrific for everyone," said Jake Kislan, director of the Drifton Complex.

The team was now 36-1 and on the backside of a tour that had taken them from coast to coast. However, the tour was not over and some of its most memorable moments were yet to come.

LEFT: *The USA team spent countless hours with their fans during the Coca-Cola USA Softball National Team Tour.*
Photo courtesy of USA Softball/Doug Hoke

One of those memorable moments occurred not on a ballfield but at Harpo Studios in Chicago where the entire team was invited to appear on the *Oprah Winfrey Show*. Not only did Ms. Winfrey pay for airline tickets and limos to the taping, she also provided complete make-overs including hair, make-up and wardrobe for the entire team. The entire nation got a glimpse of the glamorous side of the team when the segment aired as part of an Olympic preview special a couple of weeks later.

The team was involved in numerous media events as writers from the nation's most successful media made it to a tour stop or to Columbus for a few moments with the team. Included among the national television programs in which the team or athletes participated were the *Today Show, Week-end Today, Sports Illustrated for TV, the Mike and Maty Show, Live! With Regis & Kathy Lee, Crook*

& Chase, NBC's *Road to Olympic Gold* and of course, *Oprah*.

The team's afternoons in Columbus frequently became media events also as national press from all points scheduled their moment with these rising stars. Among the publications to produce features on the team or players were *USA Today, People, Newsweek,* *Time, U.S. News & World Report, Esquire, Sports Illustrated, Southern Living, Delta Sky Magazine, New York Times Magazine, TV Guide, Disney Adventures Magazine, Ladies Home Journal, Teen, Live!, Glamou*r and hundreds of others. In total over 4,000 articles were written about the team in 1996 alone.

. . . .

BOTH PAGES: *Millions read about the team in the pages of America's publications. Over 4000 stories were published on the team in 1996.*
Photos on these pages courtesy of USA Softball

Meanwhile, the team was back on the road with stops in Chattanooga, Tennessee; Akron and Ashland, Ohio; Peachtree City, Georgia and Worcester, Massachusetts. In Akron, the city's daily said it might as well have been a rock concert as over 4,000 fans of all ages filled Firestone Stadium. In Worcester, head coach Ralph Raymond was deeply moved by the recognition he received from his hometown audience.

The last leg of the tour included ten games in five cities including Bloomington, Normal, and Decatur, Illinois; St. Louis, Missouri; and a July 4 finale in Atlanta. Several local players will remember the tour for a long time including Cheryl Forgason of Bloomington who reached base on the only hit against Christa Williams. She'll remember the hit, but she'll also remember the USA's defensive play. Forgason was thrown out when a teammate attempted a bunt that was turned into a double play by Lisa Fernandez. "How often do you see a double play on a bunt?" she asked.

Bloomington Lady Hearts' second baseman Shayna Snarr took home a souvenir, a multi-colored bruise above the knee from a Fernandez pitch. To add insult to her multi-colored injury, Snarr was picked off at first on the next play by catcher Shelly Stokes. "I'm glad it left a bruise," said an admiring Snarr.

In Decatur, fans turned out from all over Illinois and as far away as Ohio, Kansas, Michigan and Tennessee. Before the first pitch, over 7,500 adoring fans gave the team a standing ovation that lasted for over five minutes as each member of the team received an emotional introduction. There were great memories associated with this stadium. Virtually every player on the USA team looked on the fans with great admiration for their devotion to promoting women's fast pitch through the years. The USA faced some of its toughest competition in Decatur, but still produced dominating results with 10-0 and 8-0 wins over the Decatur Breeze.

· · · · · · · · · · · · · · · · · · · ·

OPPOSITE PAGE (BACKGROUND): *The USA Softball tour bus.*

OPPOSITE PAGE (INSET): *Coach Raymond, talking with his troops.*

Photo courtesy of USA Softball/Doug Hoke

USA SOFTBALL NATIONAL TEAM ALTERNATES

When the International Olympic Committee (IOC) added softball to the program there were certain provisions that came with the package. One of those was to limit the size of each individual team roster to 15 players, unlike the World Championships which featured 17 and the Pan American Games with 18.

It may not seem like much to the average person, but the loss of those positions was very difficult, especially for those players who suddenly found themselves just outside the final cut. No one knows that better than the five players who were named alternates on the 1996 team. These five trained and traveled with the team for almost a year before departing just days before the start of the Olympic competition. Difficult indeed to know that you were only an eyelash from membership on America's first Olympic team.

Undaunted, but not untouched by the reality of their role, the five fulfilled their responsibilities in preparing America's team for their run to the gold. The five alternates were Jennifer Brundage of Irvine, CA; Barbara Jordan of North Hollywood, CA; Jennifer McFalls of Grand Prairie, TX; Martha O'Kelley of Las Vegas, NV; and Michelle Venturella of Bloomington, IN.

JENNIFER BRUNDAGE

Jennifer Brundage has demonstrated through her career at UCLA and in ASA women's major division play that she is among the most dangerous hitters in sports today. In 1995, Brundage set the Pac-10 record for the highest batting average (.518) and exploded for 14 home runs including two grand slams to lead the Bruins to the 1995 NCAA Women's College World Series Championship title.

Photos on these pages courtesy of USA Softball

The July 4 tour stop in Atlanta was a fitting conclusion for the tour. The scrabble games on the team bus were now over, and the writers cramps from hours of signing autographs only a memory. There would be no more early morning promotional stops or banquets to attend. It was the end of a sometimes grueling, but more often fulfilling, journey across the heartland of America.

The tour was designed to get in as many at-bats as possible and to allow the pitchers lots of work. The team had pushed themselves hard in preparation for the opening of the Olympic Games.

Competitively the tour had been successful. The USA ended with a record of 60-1 and

outscored its opponents 449-3. USA pitchers gave up only three runs in 356 innings for a team ERA of 0.08.

The tour also gave America a first look at their team; a chance to shake their hands, slap them on their backs and tell them we're with you. Many of those who attended tour games never made the journey to Atlanta. But they had their Olympic moment just the same.

My Moment will live in my Memory forever.

Although the experience had been a grueling one, the players were now no longer just great individual players, they were also a great team. "We're exhausted and we're fatigued, but we'll be 100 percent when we report to Columbus," Sheila Cornell said.

America's team had given their best by giving completely of themselves. The Olympic Games would be no different.

BARBARA JORDAN

Barbara Jordan is among the nation's most productive softball athletes with three USA gold medals, three ASA National Championship titles and three NCAA National Championships to her credit. Jordan's international success includes gold medals at the 1994 South Pacific Classic, the 1994 ISF Women's World Championship and the 1995 Pan American Games. During her college career, Jordan led Cal-State Northbridge to NCAA national titles in 1984, 1985 and 1987.

JENNIFER MCFALLS

Jennifer McFall's international debut in 1995 at the Pan American Games Qualifier in Guatemala was impressive as she batted .500 with 12 hits and 10 RBI. She picked up her second USA gold medal at Superball '95. During her college career, McFalls produced an incredible 34 game-winning hits.

MARTHA O'KELLEY

In her international debut at the 1994 ISF Women's World Championship, Martha O'Kelley led her team to their third consecutive world title. In 1995, she picked up her second USA gold medal with an impressive .438 batting performance at the 1995 Pan American Games in Argentina.

MICHELLE VENTURELLA

Michelle Venturella won every award available during her career at Indiana University, including being named to two NCAA All-American teams. In 1994, Venturella made her international debut at the Pan American Games Qualifier in Guatemala, helping the USA take the gold with a dominating 15-0 performance.

7

OLYMPIC
DREAMS
DO
COME
TRUE

The USA had trained hard since its team selection in September of 1995, including a nationwide tour of 63 games in 23 cities from April to July of 1996. Although grueling at times, the tour had been successful in taking the team to their fans and enlisting an enormous following coast to coast. Thousands were awaiting the USA's triumphant run for the gold.

But, had the tour achieved its primary goal of taking a group of 15 great individual players and molding them into one great team, a team prepared to take on the best in the world? The sport, and the USA's team in particular, had everyone's attention; now it was up to the team to make good.

The team began assembling in Columbus on July 12 about a week after their final tour date in Atlanta. The Olympic Village for softball was located about 20 minutes from the venue on the Ft. Benning army base. The setting was less than homey, but it was secure. Military police checked every bag, every credential, everyone who attempted to enter the complex. A heavy wire fence was dotted with sentries who took seriously their role in insuring that there would be no security incidents at this venue. An armed rifleman manned a position on top of the dormitories... Welcome to the Olympics.

Practice fields were located in Columbus at the South Commons complex adjacent to Golden Park. The players could see Golden Park, the venue for softball in the Olympics, from their practice area and the anticipation of what it would be like to finally march into the stadium on opening day was beginning to grow by the hour.

Each team was assigned a practice time and field by local officials of the Atlanta Committee for the Olympic Games (ACOG). The times were rotated daily under a premise of fairness to all participants. ACOG was determined to eliminate the USA's home field advantage at the Games.

Yes, everyone was elated to be in Columbus and yes, everyone appreciated the opportunity to compete in the Olympics, but there were some issues that had to be resolved. Following the USA's first practice session, they were notified by ACOG officials that they could no longer use their own practice equipment. ACOG would instead provide each team with the equipment they felt was needed for practice. They insisted that each team practice where they said and with what they provided, no exceptions.

RIGHT: *Olympic icons at Golden Park in Coumbus, Georgia.*
Photo courtesy of International Softball Federation/Bob Moreland.

OPPOSITE PAGE: *Coach Raymond talking with his team about what's ahead. Photo © 1996 Roving Trimarchi.*

The USA did take exception, insisting that the system they had used to train the team over the last year was essential to the team's success. The USA could care less what the other teams used for their practice sessions as long as everyone -- including the U.S. -- was allowed to go through their normal preparations. The ACOG's procedure was not popular with the other delegations either and they relented when the USA agreed to allow the other teams to use the U.S. equipment if desired. The equipment in question included additional protective screens that allowed the team to work on a number of skills simultaneously. The USA's practice sessions included multiple skill stations in which players would work on fielding, batting and pitching. The players would move from one station to the next during the course of the practice. The screens protected the players from stray pitches, foul tips or errant throws from another practice group in which they were not involved.

After the compromise had been reached, preparation continued on schedule. The USA had come this far, they were not going to let anyone, even ACOG, stop them from completing their mission. There was some concern about the distractions that were a part of the Olympics. There was one advantage to not being discovered, no one showed up at practice, there were no extra demands on your time and it was much easier to keep a team focused on the job at hand. But that had all changed. Media and fans had swarmed this team for months, the Olympics would only be worse. It was part of the total Olympic equation that had to be dealt with.

Part of the distraction was simply the Olympic experience itself. It was important to the athletes to associate with other athletes and go away, win or lose, with the knowledge that they had achieved something great and wonderful in their attempt.

The venue's location in Columbus posed a logistical problem for the USA. The opening ceremonies of the Olympics were to be held just two days prior to the start of the softball competition over 100 miles away in Atlanta. Each player had earned the right to be a part of this great spectacle of sport so the USA team made the trip, celebrated their Olympic moment and then dragged their weary, partied out bodies back to Columbus at 4 a.m. the following day.

Head coach Raymond understood the importance of the team's participation in the ceremonies, but he also understood that in less than 24 hours his team would be first up for a 9 a.m. command performance in the sport's Olympic debut. The team went through a final afternoon practice, made a brief appearance at a Columbus welcoming party and it was back to Ft. Benning for some rest.

Incredibly, *Sports Illustrated*'s Olympic preview magazine had picked the USA for the bronze medal in the event in total indifference to their past achievements that included the last three world titles. *SI* writer Steve Rushin corrected the error in a subsequent feature calling their Olympic picks "a brief tango with insanity." USA pitcher Michele Granger rubbed it in jokingly asking *SI* and Rushin to "kiss my gold medal."

SI had picked Canada for the gold, followed by Australia and the USA. China, unbelievably, was not even included as part of the equation.

On the morning of the competition, one columnist offered that the USA was so strong that anything less than a gold medal would be a disaster. The stands were full of former players who likely would have been Olympians also had the sport been added to the program earlier. The pressure of winning for them was also on the shoulders of the USA team. Could the USA respond not only to the challenge of the world's best competition, but also to the outside pressures that were suddenly being thrust upon them?

The USA's final stretch to the medal stand had begun.

OPPOSITE PAGE: *Michele Smith and fans.*
Photo © 1996 Robin Trimarchi.

There was considerable discussion about who would get the first start in the Olympics. There were a lot of names thrown around including Lisa Fernandez, rookie Christa Williams and Michele Smith. Some conjectured that Lisa Fernandez's Latin background would somehow influence her selection against Puerto Rico or that Williams would make her Olympic debut against what some regarded as one of the lesser teams in the competition. Michele Smith was a sentimental favorite because of her near career-ending automobile accident that occurred exactly ten years to the day of the debut game. A great storyline for the writer's covering the event, but head coach Raymond had considerations of his own.

Raymond understood fully the importance of the USA making a good showing in its inaugural game in the Olympics. Everyone was watching and the USA was expected to perform and make an early statement.

Raymond's selection of Michele Granger to start may have been a surprise to observers from afar but not to those close to the program. Raymond had demonstrated his confidence in Granger since her debut on his World Championship team in 1986 at the age of 16. In the 1995 Pan American Games, it was Granger that Raymond again relied on for four wins that included an important perfect game win over Cuba that set up the gold

LEFT: *Lisa Fernandez and Michele Smith lead the team onto the field.*

OPPOSITE PAGE: *Michele Granger's smoking pistol.*

Photos on these pages © 1996 Robin Trimarchi.

medal game for the USA. Raymond was convinced that Granger would get the USA off to the right start. And he was right.

Granger, reputed to be the world's hardest thrower, came out throwing missiles. Against Puerto Rico's first batter, Lourdes Baez, Granger came with the heat, her first pitch over the plate, the next a high riser that careened off the backstop. What appeared to be a pitch that got away, was actually Granger's not so subtle way of giving not only Baez, but her teammates also, a glimpse at the cupboard. "Expect the unexpected" was Granger's message. Granger retired Baez on strikes, allowed a bloop single by Clara Vazquez and then recorded strikeouts

two and three against Janice Parks and Jaqueline Ortiz. Granger's pistol was smoking.

In casual conversations with the media prior to the game, Dot Richardson had joked about her dream of getting the first home run in the Olympics. "I had a dream about hitting a home run on my first at-bat in the Olympics," Richardson said. Richardson has never been criticized for setting her goals too low.

Richardson did not produce a home run in her first plate appearance in the Olympics, but she did produce the first USA hit, an infield chopper that she hustled into a single. Her Pete Rose/Energizer bunny persona was already beginning to surface.

Not only did Richardson produce the USA's first hit of the Games, she also scored first after teammate Julie Smith sacrificed her to second and she

words to Live by when you play between the lines.

moved to third on a wild pitch. Richardson's UCLA buddy Lisa Fernandez, in what seemed almost by design, scored her friend with a single to right. Fernandez also scored when Kim Maher powered a double to right and Michele Smith reached on an error.

Granger resumed with a 2-0 lead going three up, three down against Puerto Rico in the second and notching two more k's.

Leah O'Brien lined out to left to start the USA second and was followed by Laura Berg, the USA's undisputed hit-by-pitch champ, who reached with her first of a tournament-record five stingers to the thigh. Richardson, perhaps still thinking about that first home run, hit into a 5-4-3 double play to end the inning.

Granger returned to the circle recording her sixth and seventh strikeouts as she again retired three consecutive batters. Granger appeared to be getting stronger as she gained more confidence with each inning pitched.

In the bottom of the third, with one out, Fernandez got things going for the USA reaching first on a hard shot up the middle. Maher followed with an almost identical shot. Cornell hit a shot off the pitcher's glove to load the bases and Michele Smith walked on four straight pitches to score Fernandez.

After the walk, Puerto Rican starter Lisa Martinez was replaced by Lisa Mize with the bases loaded. Mize was rocked by USA catcher Gillian Boxx as she singled to center field

scoring two more runs and stretching the USA lead to 5-0.

In the top of the fourth, Puerto Rico picked up their second hit of the game when Clara Vazquez singled to center field. Granger would not allow another hit the rest of the game.

Richardson, never one to waste a good dream, led off an explosive sixth inning with a home run to center field. "In my dream I actually hit it (the home run) on the first pitch of the game, but I will take them any way they come."

If the crowd was not already stirred up, by the time Richardson had rounded the bases they were in a frenzy. Richardson appeared temporarily absorbed as she attempted to embrace the mo-

A Home-Run is A Home Run is A Home-run.

game after six innings.

The USA did what was expected of them in their dominating debut against Puerto Rico, scoring 10 runs on 13 hits before the game was mercifully called in the sixth. Coach Raymond knew, however, that the USA had a long and treacherous road ahead of the them and that their testing was yet to come.

The USA was not the only team making loud statements in round one. Canada and Japan were winners in close contests with Chinese Taipei (2-1) and the Netherlands (3-0). China served notice that they were also serious about the gold with a 6-0 domination of international power-

house Australia. After one round, the USA, China, Canada and Japan were knotted at 1-0.

The USA's second contest was a repetition of the first, superpower USA against a fledgling upstart. Hit the ball, run the bases. Pitch the ball, retire the batters.

However, the Netherlands may not have fully understood

ment. Not only had the USA's offense been ignited, but also a conquering spirit that stayed with the team and their loyal entourage for the remainder of the Games.

With Fernandez on first with two outs, Cornell doubled to right field to score Fernandez. Dionna Harris, Michele Smith and Gillian Boxx also scored to end the

LEFT: *The meaning of intensity: Lisa Fernandez.*

RIGHT: *A beaming Michele Smith. Photos © 1996 Robin Trimarchi.*

their role in this drama as they mounted an early offensive attack against USA rookie Christa Williams. Williams, just months past her high school graduation, was much like teammate Michele Granger who had debuted at the World's at age 16, talented, but young — gifted, but inexperienced. Would Williams' world class arm be enough to

RIGHT: *Lori Harrigan, Julie Smith, Michele Granger.*

OPPOSITE PAGE: *Christa Williams.*

Photos on these pages © 1996 Robin Trimarchi.

balance the mental ping pong that was going on inside?

Williams has been in tough spots before. In 1995, at the Junior Girls' World Championship, she had her nose broken only two batters into an important game against China. Sensing the game could be pivotal to the team's success in the event, she refused to be relieved and struck out the next 17 batters to give the USA a 1-0 win. She contributed the win and five others as the USA took the gold medal.

Williams is confident of her ability as illustrated by an interview with John Lopez of the *Houston Chronicle*. In the article, Williams recounted an incident that happened when she was playing for Dobie High School in Houston, Texas. Seems a batter was irritated with what she had interpreted as brush off pitches by Williams. The batter at one instance screamed at Williams who responded, "If I was trying to hit you, I'd hit you in the head." Her school-girl cockiness was about to be tested.

Williams controlled the first inning, retiring her first batter and forcing a ground out and fly out of two others.

Sounds like fun.

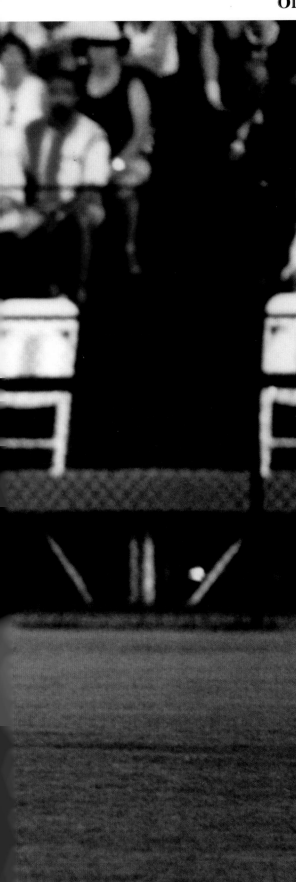

Williams survived a first-inning scare after the Netherlands' Gerardina Reijen reached base on an error by golden-glove shortstop Dot Richardson. With a runner on second and two outs, USA centerfielder Laura Berg made a spectacular diving catch in right center to snuff the threat. Four USA batters later and Williams was back in the circle.

Williams quickly dispatched the first two batters before giving up a walk to Martine Steimer. The Netherlands, sensing that opportunities would likely be few, began to swing away, delivering back-to-back singles and loading the bases. Williams was suddenly in a world-class jam.

Williams' answer? A clutch strikeout of Madelon Beek to retire the side. The drama was not over, however, as USA catcher Shelly Stokes dropped the third strike, forcing her to complete a diving tag of home plate to get the force and end the inning.

The USA bats heated up in the bottom of the second inning, scoring five runs on six hits. Sheila Cornell led off the inning with a single up the middle and then advanced to second on a passed ball. Michele Smith drove in Cornell with a single which she stretched to third when the throw from center field got away from the catcher.

Dionna Harris kept the hits coming, singling to score

I Love the feeling of Robbing Someone of their h.t.

LEFT: *Laura Berg makes a diving catch to save the day against the Netherlands.*
Photo © 1996 Robin Trimarchi.

Smith. After a sacrifice by Berg that moved Harris to second and a walk by Shelly Stokes, the USA would do even more damage. Richardson took the first pitch of her at-bat over the center field fence for her second home run of the Olympic Games to give the USA a 5-0 lead.

With a five-run cushion thanks to her teammates, Williams was beginning to feel confident that things were going to work out well for her and her team. She put the cap on her debut by retiring 15 of the next 16 batters, including 13 in a row, eight by strikeout. Not a bad debut for Houston's rising Olympic star.

Dani Tyler started things off in the fourth with a double down the left field line. Kim Maher reached on a walk and Sheila Cornell launched her first home run of the Olympic Games over the right center field fence to stretch the USA lead to 8-0.

The USA added one more run in the fifth inning when Dionna Harris singled and moved over on a fielder's choice by Stokes. Harris moved to third on a passed ball and scored on a wild pitch.

There were a host of heroes for the USA, including Dionna Harris who completed her Olympic batting debut with

three hits and a perfect 1.000 batting average. Dot Richardson and Sheila Cornell each delivered three-run bleacher reachers that put the game away. And, 18-year-old rookie Christa Williams delivered a gutsy 9-0, 0.00 ERA, two-hitter to put the USA up 2-0 heading into the third round.

There were already signs that the race for the gold was not going to be an easy one for even the favorites. In round one, Australia crumbled to China 6-0, who was then ambushed 3-0 by Japan in day two leaving only Canada, Japan and the USA unbeaten. International super-powers and medal favorites Australia and China surprisingly finished day two at 1-1.

There were some questions about round two, especially in Japan's win over China. China surprisingly started pitching ace Lihong Wang, despite her seven-inning performance only a day earlier against Australia. Unlike the Australian contest, Wang appeared to tire in the sixth and Japan took advantage scoring three runs on four singles and a walk. What made the

decision even more suspect was the fact that Lihong had withdrawn from the 1995 Asian Softball Championship due to a shoulder injury.

Michele Smith was next up for the USA against previously unbeaten Japan. Three games, three great throwers. The USA's pitching depth was beginning to surface as a major factor in the competition. Smith's pick against Japan was with some deliberation. As an employee of Toyota Corporation in Ja-

pan, Smith had played a number of seasons in the Japan League. She knew the players on the Japan team very well. They knew her very well, also.

Smith's job at Toyota involved teaching English to

executives and in the process she also became fluent in Japa-

ABOVE: *Leah O'Brien.*

RIGHT: *Julie Smith.*

OPPOSITE PAGE (TOP): *A mighty swing for the USA.*

OPPOSITE PAGE (MIDDLE): *Sheila Cornell.*

OPPOSITE PAGE (BOTTOM): *Lisa Fernandez.*
Photos © 1996 Robin Trimarchi.

showed signs of a return to softball prominence, particularly in its win over China. The Japanese had combined excellent pitching, a stingy defense and an opportunistic offense to shut down their first two opponents, outscoring them 9-0 in the process.

Japan knew that its game against the USA would be different. The USA had been equally impressive in its first two starts, outscoring the competition 19-0. The USA also knew that as it progressed into the heart of its schedule, things would likely become harder, also.

nese. She remembers that during her early playing days in Japan, "The players would yell instructions back and forth to each other while I was pitching. Since they were speaking Japanese, they thought I couldn't understand them. I let them think that for a long time." The club from Japan

The USA's contest against Japan was expected to be the team's first major obstacle in its path to Olympic gold. The Japananese have historically been among the fastest on the bases. However, their recent attempts to bunt and slap their way to the top had been less than productive. This club, however, was not only sparkling defensively, but was

hitting away and clearing the fences, recording three home runs and 11 hits in two contests.

The USA threatened again in the bottom of the second inning with a leadoff double by Laura Berg and a single by Julie Smith that put runners on the corners for Fernandez, who was at the plate. A controversial called third strike and a ground out by Maher ended the threat.

In the third inning, Naomi Matsumoto beat out a bunt to reach first and was sacrificed to second. Following a walk to Misako Ando, Smith closed the inning when Mayumi Inoue grounded out to Fernandez.

In the bottom of the third, the USA couldn't capitalize on a leadoff walk to Sheila Cornell and a single by Dionna Harris. After Gillian Boxx sacrificed to move

the runners to second and third, Leah O'Brien popped out to the shortstop for the second out of the inning. The Japanese got out of the inning when Cornell was caught in a rundown trying to score after a wild pitch.

The Japanese jumped back into the game in the fourth inning scoring one run on two hits. Japan's leadoff hitter, Haruka Saito, hit a solo home

ABOVE: *Dionna Harris.*

LEFT: *Julie Smith.*
Photos © 1996 Robin Trimarchi.

run over the right field fence to close the gap to 3-1. This was the first run given up by a USA pitcher in the Olympic competition.

The USA closed the door on any Japanese comeback in the bottom of the sixth by scoring three more runs to widen their lead to 6-1. Laura Berg reached first after being hit by a pitch for the third time in as many days. With one out, Julie Smith picked up her third hit of the day with a single to right field, which set the stage for a blast by Fernandez that cleared the fence in left field.

Smith made sure the Japanese team had no thoughts of a comeback by striking out the side in the seventh inning to give the USA the 6-1 victory.

The win over Japan pushed the USA to the top of the leader board as the only remaining undefeated team in the competition at 3-0. Japan, China and Canada trailed a game back at 2-1.

Australia, a strong pre-Olympic contender for the medals, was already in trouble by the third round after dropping a 6-0 opener to China and a 2-0 shocker to previously winless Puerto Rico.

Puerto Rico pitcher Ivelisse Echevarria managed the win even though she did not produce a single strikeout in seven innings. They scored the only runs they needed in a horrendous Australian second inning that included a triple, a double, an error, an intentional walk and a pair of wild pitches. It may be unfair to say Australia's wheels had fallen off, but their cart was without question in bad need of re-alignment. Australia replaced starting pitcher Brooke Wilkins with Melanie Roche who completed the contest with no hits and 12 strikeouts, but the 2-0 lead held up and the Australians were faced with the major challenge of being 1-2.

China also brought down previously undefeated Canada, scoring a pair of runs in the top of the first inning. Errors scored the only runs China would need as they held on to defeat Canada 2-1. Chinese pitcher Lihong Wang amazingly was brought in to pitch starter Liu Yaju out of a no-outs, bases-loaded jam in the third. It was the third consecutive game for Lihong who delivered by striking out the next two batters and then handled a line drive for the final out. Canada scored their lone run in the inning before Lihong's entrance.

There was considerable concern at the lack of television coverage of the event. NBC had filmed every contest of the game, but had produced only day-end highlights of the competition. The phones at the national offices of the Amateur Softball Association were ringing off the wall.

In a conversation on day one of the competition, an NBC producer divulged that they were scheduled to produce only two five-minute spots for the entire competition. The information resulted in calls from the International Softball Federation and the Amateur Softball Association to NBC officials in Atlanta and reciprocal promises on several occasions that a USA game would be broadcast. None of them ever were. Even months after the event's completion, editorials and complaints about NBC's coverage of softball continue to filter to the ASA.

The calls were effective, however, in eliciting additional highlight coverage. NBC was in place to cover every USA game throughout. The NBC team that stayed with softball through the event appeared enthralled by what they were experiencing and sincerely apologetic that they were unable to do more.

The matter was compounded by the fact that there was no news or sports crew on the NBC affiliate in Columbus and by policy no other affiliate from competing networks was allowed access to the competition. NBC had effectively blacked out all TV coverage of the event even though they expressed no interest in airing it themselves. Attempts to assist local TV sports teams in coverage of the event were difficult due to tough enforcement of the blackout by local ACOG officials at the venue. On numerous occasions, local sports crews were escorted not only from the stadium grounds, but from practice areas by less than hospitable ACOG volunteers.

A local news crew from WTVM-9 in Columbus had done an incredible job covering the event leading up to the Olympics, coverage that included a 30-minute documentary of the USA team and daily features on sports broadcasts for almost a year leading up to the Games. Despite their efforts, not one credential was made available to them for the Olympics.

Despite the limited TV access to the event, the success of softball's debut was hardly a secret. The print media, who had developed a bond with the USA team heading into the event, did not forget them, even if softball's cozy venue in Columbus was less than convenient for them.

For some of the media, just getting to Columbus was a challenge. By design, shuttles had been organized by ACOG to bring media to and from Atlanta. By actual application they were looked upon with significant reservation by the media, especially since the first shuttle stood up a sizeable group for the USA's debut game against Puerto Rico.

Resourceful as always, the media managed to work around an occasional snafu and attend the event in overflow numbers. The media coverage of the national tour and the Olympic

RIGHT: *Dot interview live on Today Show.*
Photo © 1996 Robin Trimarchi.

Games resulted in over 4,000 articles in the USA alone in 1996. Media interest was no longer a problem for the sport.

Softball made the most of its few cherished moments on network TV. The stars of USA Softball were becoming recognizable to the nation through NBC's nightly Olympic recaps. NBC may never understand how important these snip-its were to thousands of viewers who religiously tuned in for any scrap of softball information. The images of a smiling, jovial Dot Richardson made her an instant celebrity and an icon for not only softball, but for the Olympics as well. A live *Today Show* interview with Dot from the bleachers at Golden Park

LEFT: *USA ace Lori Harrigan, ready for battle in game four against Chinese Taipei.*

BELOW: *Dani Tyler, blowing bubbles and making plays.*

OPPOSITE PAGE: *Cornell high fives. Photos © 1996 Robin Trimarchi.*

indelibly established her as a spokesperson for the sport and women athletes throughout the world.

The USA continued its streak in day four with a 4-0 win at the hands of Lori Harrigan who allowed only two hits while striking out five in her Olympic debut.

Harrigan was in control from the outset setting down Chinese Taipei's first three batters, two on strikes, in the first inning.

The USA offense struck early in the first inning to take a 1-0 lead when Dot Richardson started things off with a walk and was sacrificed into scoring position by Dani

Tyler. Lisa Fernandez picked up the first RBI of the game with a drive to right field that scored Richardson.

Chinese Taipei managed one of only two hits during the game in the second with a single by Ching Chieh Ou to center field. With one out and a runner on first, Harrigan and company quickly extinguished any potential threat by retiring the next two batters on routine ground balls to the infield.

The USA increased their lead with a leadoff double to left field in the second inning by Michele Smith. After Dionna Harris was retired on a liner to third, Laura Berg singled to right to advance. Shelly Stokes followed with a sacrifice fly to drive in Smith and give the USA a 2-0 lead.

Chinese Taipei's next three batters flied out, struck out and popped up in the third.

The USA led off the bottom of the third with a walk to Fernandez. Julie Smith was sent in to pinch run for Fernandez, but was thrown out on the next play in a fielder's choice that put Kim Maher on first. Sheila Cornell put the game out of reach with a booming crank into the deep left field bleachers scoring herself and teammate Maher and pushing their lead to 4-0.

Cornell, among the most consistent players to have ever worn a USA uniform, was already beginning to take

control offensively. The significance of the moment was not wasted on her. At age 34, she was among the team's most battle ready and she knew that the power swats that were synonymous with her legendary career were important to the USA's success in the Games.

And, even though Richardson was clearly the emotional leader of the team, Cornell was quickly becoming the big bat

Chinese Taipei managed their second hit of the game late on a leadoff single in the sixth by Tzu Hsin Liu who was picked off moments later by USA catcher Shelly Stokes on an attempted steal of second. Harrigan retired the final five batters in order and the USA was through the first four rounds with a perfect 4-0 record heading into an important contest with Canada.

After four rounds, the USA had posted three shutouts in four games and outscored their opponents 29-1. China and Japan remained close behind at 3-1.

At 4-0 and seemingly living up to the press clippings that had already proclaimed them as champion, the USA was potentially vulnerable to a scrappy, yet eratic, Canadian club. Canada had started well with wins over Chinese Taipei (2-1) and Puerto Rico (4-0) before losing a 2-1 heartbreaker to China. Head Coach Raymond knew that the USA must remain focused. Canada had quality pitching in Lori Sippel and

ABOVE: *Fernandez with Marianne Grabavoy/ NBC.*

RIGHT: *Lori Harrigan.*

OPPOSITE PAGE (TOP): *Richardson and Julie Smith make double up at second.*

OPPOSITE PAGE (BOTTOM): *Dani Tyler turning it at second.*

Photos © 1996 Robin Trimarchi.

Karen Snelgrove, pitchers who could keep the game close. The USA would need to fire on all cylinders to keep the upset-minded Canucks in check.

The Olympics are full of distractions and retaining focus is critical, but not easy. The USA team was accustomed to wading into its fans to sign autographs and shake hands after each contest during its national team tour. The Olympics, however, was different. The USA players were playing under someone else's rules here, rules that placed the highest premium on player safety. Players, for the most part, were moved from the field, to the media interview areas and into the team bus with little direct interaction with the fans.

For some of the players, this was difficult because they felt a responsibility to thank the fans for being there...not a typical problem in today's sports environment! The dilemma was not so much on how to keep the fans away from the players, but how to keep the players away from the fans.

The USA was also concerned about being a good host in the sport's Olympic debut. The USA had already been cited for taking more than its allotted five minutes to leave the field following a game. China had protested the USA's waving to the fans upon their departure as an unfair home field advantage.

Richardson had come prepared with her own fan club, made up of her mom, dad and sister, who

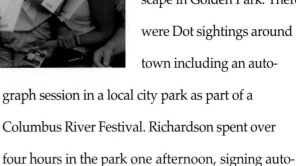

handed out fans in the shape of a softball with the inscription "I'm a Dot fan." The fans speckled the landscape in Golden Park. There were Dot sightings around town including an autograph session in a local city park as part of a Columbus River Festival. Richardson spent over four hours in the park one afternoon, signing autographs and talking with fans.

The distractions, although certainly a part of the Olympic experience, were a concern to Raymond

ABOVE: *Lisa Fernandez signing autographs.* Photo © 1996 Robin Trimarchi.

OPPOSITE PAGE: *Dot Richardson signing autographs, as Don Porter looks on.* Photo courtesy of International Softball Federation/Bob Moreland

It happens to the best of us.

and his staff who knew that the USA's lock on the gold was more media interpretation than fact...at least until it could be accomplished on the playing field.

And now, in game 5, there was also the added distraction of the weather. Rain had delayed games throughout the day including the USA's scheduled late game at 9 p.m., which did not begin until 11 p.m. A weary USA team did not leave the field until 2 o'clock the following morning. Amazingly, an overflow rain-soaked crowd of 8,645 remained for the entire contest, a testament of how important the competition was to them.

RIGHT: *Not even steady downpours could keep the fans away.*
Photo courtesy International Softball Federation/Bob Moreland

INSET: *Michele Granger.*
Photo © 1996 Robin Trimarchi.

The USA's game against Canada turned into a pitching duel as anticipated between Michele Granger and Canada's Karen Snelgrove. The USA offense looked sluggish with the order going down in sequence through three complete innings.

Canada produced the only offense early with a two-out single in the first by Christine Parris-Washington. Granger retired the side with a strikeout of Karen Doell.

Snelgrove held the USA hitless until the fourth inning when Dot Richardson singled to right field and was sacrificed to second by Julie Smith. Lisa Fernandez reached base on an errant throw by shortstop Alecia Stephenson. In a bizarre sequence of events, Canadian first baseman Carmelina Vairo fell attempting to make the catch, colliding with Fernandez. Vairo was called for obstruction and Fernandez was moved to second and Richardson allowed to score, giving the USA a precarious 1-0 lead.

Granger remained in control in the fourth, retiring the first two batters on strikes before giving up a walk and closing out with a pop-up. Through four complete innings, Granger had given up a pair of hits against 17 batters and executed seven strikeouts.

Canadian errors in the fifth allowed the USA to add another run. Michele Smith reached base on a second error by shortstop Stephenson. Gillian Boxx reached base on a fielder's choice as Canada attempted to pick off advancing runner Smith who managed to beat the throw to second. Leah O'Brien's attempted sacrifice bunt resulted in another Canadian defensive lapse which allowed her to reach

LEFT: *Gillian Boxx.*

OPPOSITE PAGE: *Julie Smith.*
Photos © 1996 Robin Trimarchi.

first, loading the bases.

With no outs and the bases full, it appeared the USA was about to make the Canadians pay big time for their defensive problems. Instead, Laura Berg hit into a fielder's choice that resulted in Smith being forced out at the plate and Dot Richardson fouled out to third. The scenario had changed and the USA was now under pressure to get something out of what seemed to be a golden opportunity to put away this pesky Canadian team and slip out of the stadium with the win. The USA managed only one run when Julie Smith delivered a single that scored Boxx.

After an inning that saw the bases loaded with no outs and USA hitters Richardson, Cornell and Maher in the wings, Snelgrove and her team must

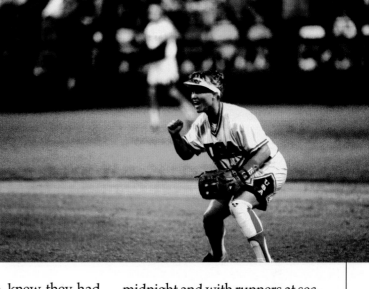

have felt fortunate to still be in this one. And, at only two runs back after five innings, they were still alive. The USA knew they had blown their opportunity to put this one in the books.

The Canadians took strength in their ability to avoid the big inning and responded with a two-run fifth of their own to tie it up at two-all. After cruising through the majority of the game, USA pitcher Michele Granger gave up three hits and two runs in the bottom of the fifth and was replaced by rookie Christa Williams.

Entering the contest well after midnight and with runners at second and third and only one out, 18-year-old Williams was about to grow up, quick. The USA's fans gasped as Williams allowed Karen Doell to reach first and load the bases after she hit to the mound and the ball rebounded off of Williams' glove.

Williams responded like a veteran, striking out Alecia Stephenson and forcing Candace Murray to fly out to left field to shut off the scoring threat.

Snelgrove retired Maher, Cornell

and Michele Smith in order in the top of the sixth and Williams reciprocated by retiring the side in the bottom.

The USA finally put the game away when Gillian Boxx singled to left field to lead off the seventh inning. Dionna Harris was brought in as a pinch runner for Boxx, who advanced to second on a walk by O'Brien.

Sensing another big inning in process, Canada replaced Snelgrove with Lori Sippel. A grounder by Laura Berg advanced

Harris and O'Brien and Harris scored when a pitch got away from catcher Carrie Flemmer to give the USA a 3-2 lead. O'Brien scored the final run of the game when Richardson doubled to left field to pick up her fifth RBI of the Olympics and give the USA a 4-2 margin heading into the bottom of the seventh.

The Canadians refused to leave quietly in the bottom of the seventh. With one out, Williams struck out Christine Parris-Washington, but she advanced after Boxx dropped the ball and failed to make the play at first. After striking out Karen Doell for the second out, the game ended dramatically when Boxx picked off Parris-Washington who was attempting to steal second.

In the fifth round, Australia was beginning to pull itself back into contention with a 10-0 thrashing of Japan. China took full possession of second, winning 8-0 against the Netherlands to improve to 4-1. The USA was 5-0, but headed into the toughest part of its schedule with consecutive games against Australia and China.

. . . .

ABOVE: *Williams and Boxx confer.*

OPPOSITE PAGE: *Play at home.*

Photos © 1996 Robin Trimarchi.

One writer called the USA's next contest against Australia the finest two hours of competition in the Olympic Games. He wasn't talking about just softball, but the Olympic Games in total. There will likely never be another Olympic game like this one.

Rain continued to be a problem. The USA had finished their 4-2 nailbiter against Canada in round five at 2 a.m. Following interviews and the drive back to the Olympic Village at Ft. Benning, it was later still. The USA team was beginning to show signs of mental and physical fatigue.

Australia had played their last game at 11:30 a.m. the previous day, giving them adequate time for rest before meeting up with the Americans at the same time a day later. Rain had delayed the first contest of the day between Japan and Puerto Rico, pushing the USA-Australia game into late afternoon. That posed additional problems for the USA team. Already in need of rest, the USA players were placed in the situation of waiting to take the field.

The USA had been saving pitcher Lisa Fernandez for this major confrontation and because of an ankle sprain earlier in the competition. "I'd play with a broken leg if I had to," Fernandez later stated in interviews.

Fernandez and Australian pitcher Tanya Harding breezed through the first inning, sitting down the side and collecting one strikeout each.

It was an interesting matchup. Fernandez, the most decorated pitcher to have ever worn a UCLA uniform, lost in her team's final game appearance in the Women's College World Series in 1993. Yet, Fernandez remains perhaps the most celebrated college player of all time. Harding, on the other hand, pitched UCLA to the national championship in 1995, and left the university and country amidst rumors that she would not return for her final exams.

Softball was in for a clash of titans. . . . .

OPPOSITE PAGE:
Fernandez. "Go ahead, Make my day."
Photo © 1996 Robin Trimarchi.

Some thought I did at regionals, no states verses ship. Still played.

In the second inning, USA first baseman Sheila Cornell picked up the first hit of the game with a single to right field and advanced to second on an error by right fielder Peta Edebone. The USA was unable to put together back-to-back hits to score Cornell and the game remained scoreless.

The USA picked up their second hit of the game in the third when Shelly Stokes singled to right field with one out. Again, the USA could not produce as Richardson grounded into a double play to end the inning.

Through four complete innings, Fernandez was winning the duel retiring twelve consecutive batters, seven on strikes. Harding faced 13, gave up two hits and produced two strikeouts.

The USA took the lead in the fifth inning when Dani Tyler delivered the hit of her lifetime into the seventh row of the center field seats. Tyler looked stunned as she rounded the bases. She was met at home plate by teammate Laura Berg who awaited with a high five. In the media tribune area located behind the backstop, television monitors recorded every play. This was a replay that no one from the USA wanted to see. Media seated in the tribune area were the first to question whether Tyler

RIGHT: *Dani Tyler rounds the bases:*
the home run that got away.
Photo © 1996 Robin Trimarchi.

had in fact touched home plate. NBC had recorded the play from several angles, each of which replayed on the monitors, each of which confirmed the error.

Had Tyler been advised by her teammates or coaches that she had missed the plate, she could have returned and corrected the error. However, by the time she had reached the dugout, the Australian team had swarmed the plate in protest. Replays had shown that the home plate umpire had not witnessed the error and the matter was deferred to the rules interpreter for the International Softball Federation, Merle Butler. Butler referred the call to the first base umpire who did not hesitate in making the reversal.

The USA team was in shock. They stood half in and half out of their dugout as Coach Raymond appealed. Dot

RIGHT: *Coach Raymond.*

OPPOSITE PAGE: *Richardson argues Tyler call.*

Photos © 1996 Robin Trimarchi.

Richardson was livid as she bolted toward the umpire who had made the call. "This is not right. The ball was in the bleachers. This is not right," she protested.

Raymond quickly removed his players and the game continued.

It was an unfortunate error, multiplied in significance by the closeness and intensity of the battle that was at hand. However, the USA, especially behind the pitching artistry of Fernandez, had every reason to believe that they would still come out victorious.

Fernandez continued to deliver and after seven innings had completed a perfect game. Now the Tyler home run was significant. Had it stood, the USA would have won the game 1-0, moved into the next round at 6-0, and Fernandez would have recorded the first perfect game in Olympic history.

After nine innings with no score, the "international tie-breaker rule" was invoked. The rule places the last batter in the previous at-bat on second base to begin the inning.

In the top of the tenth inning with Dionna Harris starting at second, Sheila Cornell hit a single to center. Haylea Petrie's throw to third bounced into the seats and Harris scored giving the USA a 1-0 lead. USA head coach Raymond appealed that Cornell should also have been awarded two bases placing her on third according to international rules, but the appeal was denied. Had Cornell been on third, the USA would likely have tried to score her on a subsequent grounder by Michele Smith.

The USA's lead appeared safe with Fernandez pitching a perfect game with 14 strikeouts headed into the bottom of the tenth. Fernandez, seemingly sensing that she was only pitches away from the win, retired Kim Cooper on strikes and Jocelyn Lester on a grounder to third. The final batter was Joanne Brown, who Fernandez had retired three times previously on strikes, a groundout and pop-up.

Fernandez was closing in on the win and Brown had two outs and two strikes in the bottom of the final inning. The USA fans had begun to move in their seats, they too sensing the inevitable USA win. Then it happened. The unspeakable. Lisa Fernandez, with the game in her pocket, delivered a riseball that failed to break and flattened out slightly over the plate. With a runner on second, Brown had nothing to lose and swung away.

ABOVE: *Australia scores winning run — with both feet.*
Photo courtesy of International Softball Federation/Bob Moreland.

OPPOSITE PAGE: *Lisa Fernandez.*
Photos © 1996 Robin Trimarchi.

The ding of the bat refocused the crowd in time for them to witness the ball as it dropped just over the center field fence.

The fans were stunned as Brown circled the bases jumping into the air and planting her feet directly into the middle of home plate. She was hoisted onto the shoulders of her teammates. Australia, who had looked dismal early on, had regrouped and done what had to be done by delivering the USA's only defeat of the Games.

The Australians and USA were gracious in victory and defeat. The USA congratulated the Australians for their victory and lavished out metaphors about winning and losing for the assembled media. But deep down this one hurt.

Fernandez fought back tears as she talked with the press afterwards as teammate Richardson attempted to console her. Young Dani Tyler took her medicine repenting of her error and winning over the media with her positive attitude. "I'm sorry it happened,

I know your pain. There are some losses that live on in your memory. And to this day, still cause chills in your spine and tears in your eyes.

but I have to put it behind me. I'm not going to let one moment define the rest of my life," she said.

The loss was a tough one for the USA, but perhaps the best possible scenario for the sport internationally. No one could forget that softball's Olympic struggles would go for naught if the sport did not remain on the program in Sydney in 2000, a decision that would not be made until months after the completion of the 1996 Games. Australian TV picked up the game in prime time and their team had risen to the occasion in front of a riveted audience that would in just four years play host themselves to the competition. Bad day for the USA. Great day for the future of international softball.

The USA could not let the loss define their destiny either as they faced perhaps their greatest test to date with a showdown against China the following day.

. . . .

BELOW: *Tyler and Fernandez at press conference. Photo © 1996 Robin Trimarchi.*

OPPOSITE PAGE: *Australians hoist Brown on shoulders after belting out game-winning home run.*
Photo courtesy of International Softball Federation/Bob Moreland.

The USA's loss to Australia had evened the playing field as China and the USA were now tied at 5-1 after six rounds. The winner of the contest would complete the round robin in first place. A resurgent Austra-lia was now back in the hunt for the medals tied with Japan at 4-2.

Many had suggested all along that the real battle for the gold was with China. After all, in the 1994 World Champion-ships and the pre-Olympic warm-up at Superball '95 it was the USA and China one and two. The USA and China had gone toe-to-toe in the past and this event would be no dif-ferent. Regardless the outcome

of the round robin match-up, the USA's road to the gold would likely head East again before it was all over.

China threatened early after USA starter Michele Smith retired the first two batters on strikes and a flyout. A single, a hit batter and a passed ball put runners on second and third, but Smith was able to get out of the inning on a foul to first base.

The USA flied out and fouled out twice to go down in order and shift the momentum back to Smith who delivered two consecutive strikeouts and a ground out to end the Chinese second.

In the bottom of the second, the USA's Kim Maher and Sheila Cornell produced back-to-back singles to lead off the

inning. Teammate Dionna Harris followed with a bunt which she beat out for a single loading the bases with no outs. A sacrifice fly by Gillian Boxx

scored Maher and Leah O'Brien reloaded the bases with a single to left field. The USA was unable to take further advantage with the final outs coming on a chopper to short that got Cornell in a force at the plate and a strikeout by

Dot Richardson.

Even though the USA had taken a slim 1-0 lead in the inning, they again were unable to take full advantage of their opportunities as they left three runners on base. Squandering what could have been a breakthrough inning for the USA, the weight shifted back to pitcher Smith who responded by retiring the next nine batters, six on strikes.

Kim Maher singled in the third and Laura Berg in the fifth, but the USA could not convert. The USA had outhit the Chinese 6-1 heading into the top of the sixth, but still led only 1-0.

· · · · · · · ·
ABOVE: *Kim Maher.*

OPPOSITE PAGE: *Cornell slide, "Eat my dirt."*

Photos © 1996 Robin Trimarchi.

The USA's inability to put China away resulted in a four-hit Chinese rally in the sixth that started on a single by leadoff batter Lu Lei. After a ground out and a pop-up, Smith was only one out from getting out of the inning with no damage until she opted for a change-up pitch that China's Xuquing Liu waited on and slapped over the fence to give the Chinese a 2-1 lead with only one inning to play.

What no one knew until after the game was that Smith had overruled the advice of coach Raymond who had specifically instructed her and catcher Gillian Boxx to stay away from the change-up on this batter. Boxx called two consecutive change-ups, the first resulting in a strike, the other a home run.

"I remember thinking to myself that I need to shake off the change-up, but I went ahead and threw the pitch anyway. I almost lost the game for

us. I knew better than that," Smith said.

Fortunately for Smith, the USA was not finished and after a walk of Kim Maher in the bottom of the sixth, Sheila Cornell returned the favor by hitting a ball into the left field bleachers to put the USA back on top at 3-2.

Smith took the Chinese down in order in the seventh, the final two batters on strikes, to secure her second win of the Olympics and give the USA the number one seed position heading into the medal rounds.

That was the good news. The bad news was that they would face number two seed China in a rematch.

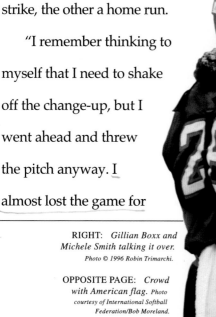

RIGHT: *Gillian Boxx and Michele Smith talking it over.*
Photo © 1996 Robin Trimarchi.

OPPOSITE PAGE: *Crowd with American flag.* Photo courtesy of International Softball Federation/Bob Moreland.

No one player wins or loses a game by themselves.

The final field of medal contenders had been determined with the USA, China, Australia and Japan all still alive and headed into the semi-final round.

USA pitcher Lisa Fernandez was spectacular in the semi-finals not allowing a hit through the first six innings and retiring 18 consecutive batters, half on strikes.

The USA offense had produced six hits during the same period including a three-hit third inning that started with a double by Dot Richardson and a single by Julie Smith. Richardson was out on the next play on a fielder's choice that moved Dionna Harris to first. With one out and runners on first and second, Kim Maher singled to right and Julie Smith was out in a close play at the plate. Sheila Cornell's chopper back to the pitcher ended the inning with the USA unable to capitalize again on a potential big inning opportunity.

The USA again threatened in the sixth with a pair of singles by Kim Maher and Gillian Boxx. However, two ground outs and a fly out ended the inning.

China launched their biggest attack of the contest with singles by Chunfang Zhang and Xuquing Liu in the top of the seventh. A sacrifice bunt, a ground out to short and a pop-up ended the threat.

China managed only one other hit in the game when Hong Chen singled to center to begin the eighth.

Fernandez produced a pair of strikeouts and a pop-up to end the inning.

The game was scoreless through the top of the tenth inning, despite the USA's hitting attack which produced nine hits. Baserunning errors in the fifth and seventh innings by the USA derailed promising scoring threats.

In the tenth with the "international tie-breaker rule" in effect, China's Xuqing Liu began the inning on second, but China was not able to take advantage as the USA retired the next three batters.

Dot Richardson began the bottom of the inning on second for the USA and was joined by Julie Smith who reached first after being hit

by a pitch. Dionna Harris loaded the bases on an error by shortstop Liu. Sheila Cornell saved the USA again by delivering the big blow for the second consecutive game when she singled to center to score Richardson and secure the win.

Fernandez ended the game with 13 strikeouts in her three-hit performance.

The win earned the USA the first spot in the gold medal final and forced China to take on the winner of the second semifinal between Australia and Japan.

In that contest, Australian right-hander Tanya Harding pitched a two-hitter to lead her team to the medal rounds by eliminating Japan 3-0. Home runs by Haylea Petrie in the fifth and Kerry Dienelt in the seventh were the difference.

The USA was again in the driver's seat, ticket already in hand for entrance to the sport's most historic game ever, the Olympic gold medal final. China and Australia would have to scratch their way through two wins tomorrow if they were going to usurp the USA's golden mission. The USA was finally in control of their own destiny.

After all the upsets and surprises throughout the week, the final three combatants were as expected. The USA, China and Australia finished one-two-three at the 1994 World Championships and at Superball '95, and after the dust had settled, here they were making their claim for the medals again, this time in the Olympics.

China took the early lead in the second on a home run by Wang Ying. Australia responded immediately with two runs of their own in the bottom of the inning to take a 2-1 lead.

China tied the game in the fourth inning on a double by Xuquing Liu and an RBI single by Hong Chen.

With the game knotted at 2-2 through four innings, China produced the game-winning run in the fifth when Zhang Chunfang doubled and later scored following a hit batter, a walk and a passed ball. Chunfang scored again in the seventh on a single, a passed ball and an error by shortstop Kim Cooper.

The Australian team that had earned its way to the medal rounds with spectacular play in the latter games of the preliminaries had once again become the team that went 1-2 in the early rounds, beating themselves with errors, passed balls and missed opportunities. China's workhorse pitcher Lihong Wang completed her seventh game of the competition.

This was not Australia's event even though they showed brilliance during their high points. They also endeared themselves to the fans with their warmth and sportsmanship throughout the

. . . .

OPPOSITE PAGE: *Lisa Fernandez and teammates celebrate.*
Photo © 1996 Robin Trimarchi.

competition. Whether it was the ecstasy of victory or the agony of defeat, the ladies of Australia proved themselves qualified ambassadors for the sport.

USA Softball's long-standing dream of becoming the first to capture Olympic gold was about to become a reality.

A capacity crowd filled Golden Park for the final game of the 1996 Olympic Games. The juggernauts of international softball, the USA and China, after more than a week of struggles and hard-fought competition, had one last game to play.

Concerns about softball's public reception in its debut

were gone. The USA had played to overflow crowds in every contest, in beautiful sunshine at midday or downpours in the early morning, it made no difference, whenever the players were on the field, the fans were in their seats.

There were many new faces among the media in attendance representing the most recognizable news outlets in the industry —new converts for a sterling group of young athletes who were giving some of these writers their first glimpse of a genuine Olympic moment.

ABOVE: *Many, including these Columbus Volunteers, worked diligently in anticipation of the event.*
Photo courtesy of International Softball Federation/Bob Moreland

There were many friends and welcome faces also. Writers such as Mark McDonald, *Dallas Morning News*; Mike DeArmond, *Kansas City Star*; Bonnie Desimoni, *Chicago Tribune*; Al Young, *USA Today*; Molly Blue, *Columbus Ledger-Enquirer*; Joe Earle, *Atlanta Journal-Constitution*; Tom Saladino, *Associated Press*; and Bill Buchalter, *Orlando Sentinel* who had stayed the course and befriended these athletes not just when their story became headlines, but when no one else was much interested in talking to them. The sport of softball and the USA team in specific owes a lot to these professionals who in the course of doing their jobs became friends and well-wishers and who helped take the sport's athletes from the shadows to the spotlight.

It was incredible to think, but the USA's moment of destiny was no longer approaching, it had arrived. Everything that thousands of players, administrators and fans had worked and longed for was happening. It was the USA's time to seize the opportunity.

The event completed its sell-out run with another overflow audience of 8,750. Ticket seekers were lined up for miles at the entrance to the facility, but there were few, even at scalper's prices, who would part with their ticket to history. Golden Park was one venue in which commercialism placed well behind the unfolding human drama taking place on the playing field.

Michele Granger had started the competition for the USA and now she was being called on to complete it as well, dominating early as she retired four batters on strikes in the first two innings.

In the bottom of the first inning, Richardson led off with a single, but was out on a fielder's choice. Lisa Fernandez flied out and Kim Maher went down looking to retire the side.

China and the USA went down in order in the second. Two innings gone and the gold medal was still up for grabs.

China challenged in the top of the third with two outs starting with a single to right field by Chunfang Zhang. Teammate Fang Yan followed with a single and then on the next play attempted to steal second. Catcher Gillian Boxx's pick-off throw to second missed Yan, but shortstop Dot Richardson came back to Boxx with a bullet that picked off Zhang who was attempting to

RIGHT: *Boxx defending her plate.*

OPPOSITE PAGE: *Granger...the look says it all.*
Photos © 1996 Robin Trimarchi.

score. Zhang was called out at the plate even though TV replays seemed to suggest that her leg may have gotten under Boxx ahead of the tag. Even after repeated replays it was a 50/50 call on whether she was out or safe. Whatever, the call went with the USA who was purposed not to let any chance pass them by in this game.

It was time to make a move and Laura Berg obliged with an important leadoff single that brought up the top of the order and USA leadoff hitter Dot Richardson.

Berg prepared herself at first, glancing nervously back and forth between second and the plate. Every play was beginning to take on increased significance as the game moved forward.

Richardson's bead was on every pitch of China's Yaju Liu. She repeatedly stepped out of the box stretching and bouncing before stepping back in, seemingly trying to settle down the emotions that were beginning to flow in on her.

Several softball stars from Richardson's past speckled the backdrop behind her including Joan Joyce, Sharron Backus, Irene Shea, Diane Davidson, Mary Lou Cushing, Kathy Arendsen, Bertha Tickey, Stephanie Tenney and Judy Hall. During the warm-up before the game, Hall had tossed Richardson a softball from the stands. Richardson had signed so many softballs during the week for fans that she immediately reached for a pen until she realized they had signed

LEFT: *Richardson celebrates home run.*

OPPOSITE PAGE: *Fernandez clings to the bag.*

Photos © 1996 Robin Trimarchi.

bases to a deafening chorus of "USA-USA." It was only the third inning, but everyone sensed that this was the end of the journey.

China protested the home run, contending that the ball had gone foul just before exiting. Replays clearly indicated that even though the ball was slicing toward foul territory in its final trajectory, it had in fact left the field a good foot inside the foul pole. The ISF umpire who made the preliminary call was only a few yards from the ball on its exit and in perfect position to make the determination.

Despite a protest that lasted over ten minutes, this time the run stayed on the

the ball for her. They were symbolically letting her know that she was playing this game for them also.

Richardson had made the most of her prime-time moments throughout the competition and this was clearly one of them.

Stepping in to take Liu's delivery, Richardson connected, driving the pitch deep into the right field corner. Chinese rightfielder Qiang Wei, obviously caught off guard by the blast, twisted and turned trying to position herself to make a play on the ball at the fence. It was too late and the ball too deep. Wei stood pointing at the ball that came to its final rest behind the fence in foul territory.

Meanwhile, Berg and Richardson rounded the

hit to center that was bobbled pushing the USA's lead to 3-0.

Granger retired the next seven batters before giving up a single to Zhang and a double to Xuquing Liu in the sixth. With runners

board and the USA was up 2-0. They added an additional run after Julie Smith reached first on an error by Chinese third baseman Hua Tao. Lisa Fernandez then reached on a fielder's choice that retired Smith. Kim Maher reached on a fielder's choice that retired Fernandez and then scored when Sheila Cornell followed with a

at second and third and two outs, Raymond was taking no chances of letting China crawl back into this one on a late-inning rally and replaced Granger with Fernandez.

The crowd cringed when Fernandez's first pitch turned into a passed ball that scored China's lone run. Fernandez was not about to allow history to repeat itself as she blew pitches by Chinese batter Ying Wang who was caught looking.

Unable to score in the bottom of the sixth, the USA moved into the seventh with a 3-1 lead behind the pitching of perhaps the best closer in the game in Fernandez. The championship was the USA's for the taking.

Fernandez retired the first batter on a ground out, the second on strikes. The gold was now on the line. It had all come down to a final battle between Fernandez and China's pinch hitter Jian Xu. And then it was down to one pitch. When Fernandez fired the final strike, gloves began to fly into the air in celebration. Fernandez was on springs as she repeatedly boinged herself into midair knee bends before landing in the outstretched arms of batterymate Gillian Boxx. Moments later the entire team and coaches were crumpled in an infield pile of twisted bodies and high fives.

The crowd had been on their feet since Fernandez's final strike had blown past the Chinese batter and the plate umpire had signaled the game's conclusion. Unpiling, the USA team began to make their way to the fringes of the field to wave and celebrate with friends, family and thousands of softball fans.

. . . .

LEFT: *Dot Richardson.*

BACKGROUND: *Michele Smith and Richardson hug.*

OPPOSITE PAGE(TOP): *Maher beats the throw.*

OPPOSITE PAGE(BOTTOM): *Granger making point to Fernandez.*
Photos © 1996 Robin Trimarchi.

The team made their final tribute to fans nationwide as they were interviewed on live TV by NBC Olympic anchor Bob Costas. The image of the team's jubilant response to Costas' questions remains a golden moment for the sport and its new Olympic champions.

Moments later the USA team was on the stand receiving their gold medals in recognition of their remarkable achievement. Smiles were abundant as each athlete

had her personal moment of Olympic glory, first the flowers, then the medal, followed by a waving salute to the thousands who remained to relish the moment with the athletes. The smiles turned to tears as the players refocused themselves and in solidarity turned again as a team to watch as the national flags of the medal winners slowly emerged in the background. By the time the national anthem of the United States was complete, tears were streaming down the faces of the

ABOVE: *The whole team takes a bow.*
Photo © 1996 Mike Hewitt/All Sport USA.

athletes who must have realized in an instant that they had become representatives not only for themselves and their sport, but for their nation as well.

Softball's triumphant run to the first Olympics was over. They had crowned their first champion. The USA had completed its mission and captured the gold.

The individuals who made the opportunity happen were many. They included thousands of volunteers and players. The Amateur Softball Association and the International Softball Federation set the course and worked the plan that finally delivered the opportunity. The players of the world stepped up to the challenge and took full advantage.

The process was long and difficult and there were mistakes made along the way. After all, every step was a new step for the sport and there was no pattern to follow. Through it all, the results were worth the effort.

This was not a perfect Olympics and the USA team was not a perfect team. However, it was a tremendously gratifying and successful debut for the sport.

It was a debut that managed to embrace almost everyone. This was softball's first birthday in the Olympics and everyone was invited to the party.

There will never be another Olympics like this one for the sport. Firsts are always like that. But, the future of the sport looks more promising than ever as it moves toward the 2000 Games in Sydney, Australia.

The USA team that prepared themselves aptly for their moment of destiny will forever remain *Etched in Gold* in our memory.

When the trumpets summon the heroes of the 2000 Games, softball's best will gratefully be among those ready to respond.

. . . .

OPPOSITE PAGE: *National anthem.*
Photo © 1996 Robin Trimarchi.

USA Softball

Batting and Fielding Statistics for 1996 Olympic Games

NAME	G	POS	BA	AB	H	R	RBI	HR	TB	SLG%	OB%	BB	HP	SO	PO	E	FLD%
Berg	9	CF	.273	22	6	2	0	0	7	.318	.383	0	5	0	9	0	1.000
Boxx	6	C	.250	16	4	2	3	0	5	.312	.200	0	0	3	73	0	1.000
Cornell	9	1B	.393	28	11	5	9	3	22	.786	.469	4	0	4	51	1	.981
Fernandez	9	3B	.348	23	8	5	5	1	11	.478	.464	5	0	2	3	0	1.000
		P													1	0	1.000
Granger	3	P	.000	0	0	0	0	0	0	.000	.000	0	0	0	0	0	.000
Harrigan	1	P	.000	0	0	0	0	0	0	.000	.000	0	0	0	0	0	1.000
Harris	9	RF	.409	22	9	5	1	0	9	.409	.458	1	1	1	1	0	1.000
		DH													0	0	.000
		PR													0	0	.000
Maher	9	LF	.219	32	7	7	3	1	11	.344	.265	2	0	5	5	1	.833
O'Brien	7	RF	.300	10	3	1	0	0	3	.300	.385	2	0	1	2	0	1.000
		PR													0	0	.000
Richardson	9	SS	.273	33	9	7	7	3	20	.606	.306	2	0	6	12	1	.962
Smith, J.	7	2B	.238	21	5	2	1	0	5	.238	.280	1	1	1	11	0	1.000
		PR													0	0	.000
Smith, M.	9	P	.211	19	4	3	2	0	5	.263	.250	1	0	1	0	0	1.000
		DH													0	0	.000
		PR													0	0	.000
Stokes	3	C	.167	6	1	1	1	0	1	.167	.333	2	0	1	31	0	1.000
Tyler	7	2B	.167	18	3	1	0	0	7	.389	.158	0	0	4	1	0	1.000
		3B													3	0	1.000
		PR													0	0	.000
Williams	2	P	.000	0	0	0	0	0	0	.000	.000	0	0	0	0	1	.667
Team Totals:	9		.280	250	70	41	32	8	106	.424	.337	20	7	29	200	4	.985

Pitching Statistics for 1996 Olympic Games

NAME	L/R	GP	GS	W	L	ERA	IP	H	R	ER	HR	BB	SO	HP	WP
Fernandez	R	9	9	1	1	0.33	21.0	4	2	1	1	0	31	0	0
Granger	L	3	3	2	0	0.87	16.0	11	2	2	0	5	25	0	1
Harrigan	L	1	1	1	0	0.00	7.0	2	0	0	0	0	5	0	0
Smith, M.	L	9	8	2	0	1.50	14.0	8	3	3	2	3	23	1	0
Williams	R	2	1	2	0	0.00	9.2	3	0	0	0	2	15	0	0
Team Totals		9	9	8	1	0.62	67.2	28	8	6	3	10	99	1	1

CITIUS · ALTIUS · FORTIUS

INTERNATIONAL OLYMPIC COMMITTEE

SPORTS DEPARTMENT

BY FAX : Code 028

Mr. Don E. PORTER
President
Fédération Internationale de Softball
(ISF)
2801 N.E. 50th St.
Oklahoma City,
OKLAHOMA 73111-7203
USA

Lausanne, 13th December 1996
Ref. No   **4476** /96/pmu

Re: Olympic programme

Dear Mr. Porter,

   We have pleasure in informing you that the IOC Executive Board, at its meeting held in Cancun on 15th November 1996, decided to keep women's Softball, on a provisional basis, in the programme of the Games of the XXVII Olympiad, Sydney 2000.

   We hope that this will help you to work towards the development of your sport worldwide.

                          Yours sincerely,

                          Gilbert FELLI
                          Sports Director

HONOR

ROLL

The following listing includes players who have represented the USA in a variety of international events beginning at the I ISF Women's World Championship in 1965. This section is dedicated to each of those players who contributed to softball's growth and development and ultimately its arrival on the Olympic Games program.

BACKGROUND: *USA Softball Top Guns Lisa Fernandez, Susie Parra, Michele Smith, Lori Harrigan and Debbie Doom. Taken before the 1993 Intercontinental Cup in which they dominated 9-0 and posted a team ERA of 0.00.*
Photo courtesy of USA Softball

I ISF WOMEN'S WORLD CHAMPIONSHIP

February 13-21, 1965   Melbourne, Australia

USA TEAM *Silver Medalists*
William S. Simpson, general manager
Vincett Devitt, manager
Anna DeLuca
Millie Dubord
Laura Malesh
Brenda Reilly
Bertha Tickey
Donna Lopiano
Pat Harrison
Kathryn "Sis" King
Mickey Stratton
Edna Fraser
Beverly Danaher
Mary Bennett
Carol La Rose

II ISF WOMEN'S WORLD CHAMPIONSHIP

August 22-30, 1970   Osaka, Japan

USA TEAM MEMBERS *Silver Medalists*
Carol Spanks, player-manager
Shirley Topley, player-coach
Rosalie Sorenson, coach
Mary Lou Adams
Rosie Adams
Sherron Bredeen
Mickey Davis
Karel Graham
Nance Ito
Cecilia Ponce
Jackie Rice
Pattie Schnell
Sue Sims
Carol Spanks
Shirley Topley
Nancy Welborn
Roxanne Zavala

III ISF WOMEN'S WORLD CHAMPIONSHIP

August 8-16, 1974   Stratford, Connecticut

USA TEAM *Gold Medalists*
Ralph Raymond, team manager/coach
John Stratton, team manager/coach
Rose Marie Adams
Sharron Backus
Joann Cackowski
Barbara Clark
Joyce Compton
Kathy Elliott
Joan Joyce
Peggy Kellers
Joan Moser
Cecilia Ponce
Willie Roze
Irene Shea
Clair Tomasiewicz
Susan Tomko
Pat Whitman

IV ISF WOMEN'S WORLD CHAMPIONSHIP

October 12-21, 1978   San Salvador, El Salvador

USA TEAM *Gold Medalists*
Ralph Raymond, head coach
Barbara Reinalda
Joan Van Ness
Gina Vecchione
Sue Enquist
Kathy Strahan
Marilyn Rau
Pat Fernandes
Doreen Denman
Barbara Clark
Kathy Arendsen
Diane Schumacher
Constance Clabby
Lana Svec
Beth Quesnel

V ISF WOMEN'S WORLD CHAMPIONSHIP

July 2-11, 1982 Taipei, Taiwan

USA TEAM
Fourth Place
Marge Ricker, Coach
Marcia Newsome
Darlene Lowery
Melissa Coulter
Patty Pyle
Snooki Mulder
Lindd James
Lou Piel
Sandra Loveless
Shirley Burton
Kathy Stilwell
Tracy Compton
Jae Butera
Dot Richardson
Amy Lyons
Joanne Blackford
Debbie Doom

VI ISF WOMEN'S WORLD CHAMPIONSHIPS

January 18-27, 1986   Auckland, New Zealand

USA TEAM *Gold Medalists*
Ralph Raymond, head coach
Dot Richardson
Jackie Gaw
Kristen Peterson
Lisa Ishikawa
Allyson Rioux
Elizabeth O'Conner
Michele Granger
Deanne Moore
LeAnn Jarvis
Trish Mang
Chris Dinoto
Jenea Lambdin
Gretchen Larson
Doreen Denman
Pat Dufficy
Kathy Arendsen
Barbara Reinalda

BELOW: *1994 World Champions*
Photo courtesy of USA Softball

VII ISF WOMEN'S WORLD CHAMPIONSHIP

July 14-21, 1990   Normal, Illinois

USA TEAM *Gold Medalists*

Ralph Raymond, Head Coach
Roger Dawes, Assistant Coach
Shirley Topley, Assistant Coach
Sheila Cornell
Pam Newton
Kris Peterson
Dot Richardson
Mary Lou Flippen
Jill Justin
Denise Eckert
Xan Silva
Suzy Brazney
Lee Ann Jarvis
Karen Sanchelli
Tammy Hollaway
Becky Duffin
Debbie Doom
Lisa Longaker
Lisa Fernandez
Kathy Arendsen

VIII ISF WOMEN'S WORLD CHAMPIONSHIP

July 30-August 1, 1994
St. John's, Newfoundland, Canada

USA TEAM *Gold Medalists*

Ralph Raymond, head coach
Mike Candrea, assistant coach
Margie Wright, assistant coach
Carol Spanks, assistant coach
Laura Berg
Gillian Boxx
Jenny Condon
Sheila Cornell
Pat Dufficy
Lisa Fernandez
Michele Granger
Michelle Gromacki
Lori Harrigan

Barbara Jordan
Jill Justin
Martha O'Kelley
Susie Parra
Dot Richardson
Karen Sanchelli
Julie Smith
Michele Smith

1979 PAN AM GAMES

July 1-15, 1979   San Juan, Puerto Rico

USA TEAM *Gold Medalists*

Ralph Raymond, head coach
Lorene Ramsey, assistant coach
Marilyn Rau
Julie Winklepleck
Kathy Arendsen
Melannie Kyler
Paula Noel
Diane Schumacher
Dot Richardson
Joan Van Ness
Kathy Strahan
Gwen Berner
Shirley Mapes
Sue Enquist
Sylvia Ortiz
Brenda Marshall
Paula Stufflebeam
Suzie Gaw
Barbara Reinalda
Linda Spagnola

1983 PAN AMERICAN GAMES

August 15-26, 1983   Caracas, Venezuela

USA TEAM *Silver Medalists*

Ralph Raymond, head coach
Lorene Ramsey, assistant coach
Kathy Arendsen
Suzy Brazney
Sheila Cornell
Pat Dufficy

Suzie Gaw
Venus Jennings
Darlene Lowery
Missy Mapes
Deanne Moore
Starleen Orullian
Barbara Reinalda
Dot Richardson
Allyson Rioux
Diane Schumacher
Wendy Smith
Lori Stoll
Gina Vecchione
Pam Warner

1987 PAN AM GAMES

August 7-19, 1987 Indianapolis, Indianna

USA TEAM *Gold Medalists*
Carol Spanks, head coach
Linda Wells, assistant coach
Karen Sykes, manager
Annette Ausseresses
Lisa Baker
Denise Carter
Kathy Escarcega
JoAnn Ferrieri
Suzie Gaw
Suzy Brazney
Mary Mizera
Vicki Morrow
Donna McElrea
Elizabeth O'Connor
Catharine Stedman
Alison Stowell
Dot Richardson
Ella Vilche
Rhonda Wheatley
Michele Granger
Sheila Cornell

1991 PAN AM GAMES

August 3-12, 1991 Santiago de Cuba, Cuba

USA TEAM *Gold Medalists*
Shirley Topley, head coach
Margie Wright, assistant coach
Barbara Booth
Suzy Brazney
Sheila Cornell
Denise Day
Brenda Dobbelaar
Debbie Doom
Lisa Fernandez
Suzie Gaw
Michele Granger
Debbie Hoddevik
Mindy Jenkins
Patricia Johnson
Jill Justin
Ann Rowan

1995 PAN AM GAMES

March 13-25 Parana, Argentina

USA TEAM *Gold Medalists*
Ralph Raymond, head coach
Ralph Weekly, Jr., assistant coach
Shirley, Topley, assistant coach
Patti Benedict
Jenny Condon
Sheila Cornell
Debbie Doom
Pat Dufficy
Michele Granger
Lori Harrigan
Barbara Jordan
Jill Justin
Kim Maher
Martha O'Kelley
Susie Parra
Dot Richardson
Ann Rowan
Karen Sanchelli
Julie Smith
Michele Smith
Shelly Stokes

OTHER EVENTS

I TRI-NATION CHAMPIONSHIP

September 3-13, 1981 Osaka, Japan

USA TEAM *Gold Medalists*
Marge Ricker, Coach
Patty Pyle
Lou Piel
Dot Richardson
Kathy Arendsen
Sue Enquist
Lori Stoll
Patty Cutright
Debbie Doom
Marilyn Rau
Barb Garcia
Lisa Clinchy
Starleen Orullian
Sue Lewis
Sue Kragseth
Mary Owen

II TRI-NATION CHAMPIONSHIP

July 16-August 1, 1985 Beijing, China

USA TEAM *Silver Medalists*
Cyndi Watson, coach
Bobbi Jordan, manager
Sue Lewis
Pam Edde
Debby Langevain
Sheila Cornell
Pam Reindehl
Patti McCoy
Sue Bristow
Jerry Nedra
Tobi Perkins
Stacy Winsberg
Angie LoSasso
Leslie King

III TRI-NATION CHAMPIONSHIP

July 7-10, 1988 Oklahoma City, Oklahoma

USA TEAM *Gold Medalists*
Carol Spanks, coach
Shirley Topley, coach
Julie Smith
Barbara Garcia
Suzy Brazney
Susan Le Febvre
Debbie Doom
Nicky Luce
Kim Nutter
Lori Peterson
Julie Parmenter
Michele Granger
Suzie Gaw
Donna McElrea
Janice Parks

IV TRI-NATION CHAMPIONSHIP

June 14-16, 1992 Izumo, Japan

USA TEAM *Silver Medalists*
Kathy Arendsen
Suzy Brazney
Sheila Cornell
Denise Correa
Lisa Erickson
Lisa Fernandez
Rina Foster
Lori Harrigan
Jill Justin
Cheri Kempf
Jennae Lambdin
Dot Richardson
Kris Schmidt
Michele Smith
Julie Smith
Shay Sodano
Charlotte Wiley

BACKGROUND: *1988 Tri-Nation Champions*
Photo courtesy of USA Softball

1985 SOUTH PACIFIC CLASSIC
March 9-17, 1985 Melbourne, Australia

USA TEAM *Gold Medalists*
Carol Spanks, coach
Linda Wells, coach
Sue Lewis
Diane Schumacher
Pam Reinoehl
Karen Fellenz
Dot Richardson
Pat Dufficy
Kay Piper
Carol Maioran
Tracy Beadlescomb
Linda Thaler
Mary Wisniewski
Kris Bergstrom
Marilyn Rau
Sue Brazney
Tracy Compton
Debbie Doom
Kathy Van Wyke
Barbara Reinalda

1989 SOUTH PACIFIC CLASSIC
February 3-12, 1989
Christchurch, New Zealand

USA TEAM *Fourth Place*
Roger Dawes, coach
Lisa Baker
Suzy Brazney
Tracey Compton
Cindy Cooper
Sheila Cornell
Tammy Delp
Suzie Gaw
Kari Johnson
Barbara Jordan
Debby Langevain
Pam Newton
Terri Oberg
Chenita Rogers
Kathy Van Wyk

BELOW: *1994 South Pacific Classic Champions*
Photo courtesy of USA Softball

1994 SOUTH PACIFIC CLASSIC

April 21-25, 1994 Sydney, Australia

USA TEAM *Gold Medalists*
Ralph Raymond, head coach
Shirley Topley, assistant coach
Carol Sparks, assistant coach
Jenny Condon
Cindy Cooper
Sheila Cornell
Pat Dufficy
Susie Gaw
Michele Granger
Michelle Gromacki
Lori Harrigan
Barbara Jordan
Jill Justin
Trish Popowski
Karen Sanchelli
Julie Smith
Karen Walker

1984 WOMEN'S INTERNATIONAL CUP

June 29-July 4, 1984 El Monte, CA

USA TEAM *Gold Medalists*
Ralph Rayond, manager
Andy Van Etter, coach
Kathy Arendsen
Barbara Reinalda
Doreen Denmon
Regina Dooley
Diane Schumacher
Gretchen Larson
Allison Rioux
Missy Mapes
Dot Richardson
Jackie Gaw
Chris Dinoto
Deanna Moore
Gina Vecchione
Elizabeth Luckie
Rehe Clark
Kristen Peterson
Julie Buldoz

1992 WORLD CHALLENGER CUP

June 21-28, 1992 Beijing, China

USA TEAM *Gold Medalists*
Ralph Raymond, head coach
Shirley Topley, assistant coach
Kathy Arendsen
Suzy Brazney
Sheila Cornell
Denise Correa
Lisa Erickson
Lori Harrigan
Cheri Kempf
Barbara Jordan
Jill Justin
Jennae Lambdin
Lisa Fernandez
Sara Foster
Dot Richardson
Kristin Schmidt
Julie Smith
Michele Smith
Sharon Sodano
Charlotte Wiley

BELOW: *1984 Women's International Cup Champions*
Photo courtesy of USA Softball

1993 INTERCONTINENTAL CUP

July 17-25, 1993 Haarlem, Holland

USA TEAM *Gold Medalists*
Ralph Raymond, head coach
Shirley Topley, assistant coach
Suzy Brazney
Sheila Cornell
Lisa Fernandez
Lori Harrigan
Jill Justin
Rachel Brown
Debbie Doom
Dionna Harris
Kelly Jackson
Janice Parks
Trisha Popowski
Christine Serritella
Karen Walker
Susie Parra
Ann Rowan
Priscilla Rouse

ABOVE: *1993 Intercontinental Cup Champions*
Photo courtesy of USA Softball

PAN AM QUALIFIER

December 8-17, 1994
Guatemala City, Guatemala

USA TEAM *Gold Medalists*
Ralph Weekly, Jr., head coach
Sue Enquist, assistant coach
Diane Schumacher, assistant coach
Holly Aprile
Gillian Boxx
Heather Compton
Jennifer Dalton
Lisa Fernandez
Gina Givogri
Michelle Gromacki
Dionna Harris
Beth Kirchner
Jennifer McFalls
Leah O'Brien
Trish Popowski
Eileen Schmidt
Bonnie Tholl

Dani Tyler
Michelle Venturella
Dee Dee Weiman
Christa Williams

SUPERBALL '95

August 3-6, 1995 Columbus, GA

USA TEAM *Gold Medalists*
Ralph Raymond, head coach
Ralph Weekly, assistant coach
Margie Wright, assistant coach
Laura Berg
Jenny Condon
Sheila Cornell

Lisa Fernandez
Michele Granger
Michelle Gromacki
Jill Justin
Kim Maher
Jennifer McFalls
Leah O'Brien
Martha O'Kelley
Trish Popowski
Dot Richardson
Michele Smith
Shelly Stokes
Dani Tyler
Dee Dee Weiman

ABOVE: *Dee Dee Weiman at Superball '95.*
Photo courtesy of USA Softball/Doug Hoke.

1995 U.S. OLYMPIC FESTIVAL WOMEN'S ROSTERS

SOUTH TEAM
Patti Benedict, Wyoming, MI
Laura Berg, Santa Fe Springs, CA
Jennifer Brundage, Irvine, CA
Nikki Cockrell, Pasadena, TX
Sheila Cornell, Burbank, CA
Jenny Dalton, Glendale, CA
Debbie Doom, El Monte, CA
Michelle Gromacki, Antioch, CA
Lori Harrigan, Las Vegas, NV
Shari Johnson, Glendale, AZ
Beth Kirchner, Sioux City, IA
Martha O'Kelley, Las Vegas, NV
Christa Saindon, Cerritos, CA
Lidia Stiglich, Albany, CA
Christa Williams, Houston, TX
Coach: Ralph Weekly, Jr, Chattanooga, TN

NORTH TEAM
Julie Adams, Cypress, CA
Jen Babik, Piscataway, NJ
Pat Dufficy, Stratford, CT
Lisa Fernandez, Long Beach, CA
Whitney Floyd, San Jose, CA
Barbara Jordan, Huntington Beach, CA
Nina Lindenberg , Anaheim Hills, CA
Susie Parra, Scottsdale, AZ

Kim Rondina, Scottsdale, AZ
Julie Smith, Glendora, CA
Shelly Stokes, Carmichael, CA
Tiff Tootle, Reidsville, GA
Michelle Venturella, Bloomington, IN
Karen Walker-Deegan, Woodland Hills, CA
Tiffany Whittall, Oklahoma City, OK
Coaches: Mike Candrea, Casa Grande, AZ
Diane Schumacher, Rock Island, IL

EAST TEAM
Holly Aprile, Charleston, IL
Leah Braatz, Costa Mesa, CA
Michelle Bolster, St. Petersburg, MI
Jill Justin, Oak Lawn, IL
Cheri Kempf, Brentwood, TN
Kim Maher, Fresno, CA
Sara Mallett, Whittier, CA
Jennifer McFalls, Grand Prairie, TX
Missy Nowak, Chicago, IL
Cyndi Parrus, Covina, CA
Lori Reese, Shippensburg, PA
Priscilla Rouse, Lakeview Terrace, CA
Ann Rowan, Phoenix, AZ
Eileen Schmidt, Barto, PA
Dee Dee Weiman, Los Angeles, CA
Coaches: Margie Wright, Fresno, CA
Sue Enquist, Los Angeles, CA

WEST
Gillian Boxx, Torrance, CA
Susie Bugliarello, Sunnyvale, CA
Heather Compton, Santa Maria, CA
Jenny Condon, Edina, MN
Gina Givogri, Elk Grove, CA
Dionna Harris, Wilmington, DE
Alison Johnsen, Irvine, CA
Leah O'Brien, Chino, CA
Trish Popowski, Laurence Harbor, NJ
Dot Richardson, Orlando, FL
Karen Sanchelli, Columbia, SC
Rachel Shipley, Wheaton, IL
Michele Smith, Plainfield, NJ
Dani Tyler, Des Moines, IA
Ali Viola, Novato,CA
Coaches: Shirley Topley, Anaheim, CA
Carol Spanks, Henderson, NV

OLYMPIC TEAM CAMP
August 31-September 4, 1995
Oklahoma City, Oklahoma

Athletes invited to the USA Softball Olympic Team Camp in state order included the following:

ALASKA:
Michele Granger, Anchorage

ARIZONA:
Suzie Gaw, Scottsdale
Shari Johnson, Glendale
Susie Parra, Scottsdale
Kim Rondina, Scottsdale
Ann Rowan, Phoenix

CALIFORNIA:
Laura Berg, Santa Fe Springs
Gillian Boxx, Torrance
Jenny Brewster, Cerritos
Jennifer Brundage, Irvine
Susie Bugliarello, Sunnyvale
Amy Chellevold, Thousand Oaks
Heather Compton, Santa Maria
Sheila Cornell, Diamond Bar
Jenny Dalton, Glendale
Lisa Daquisto, Westminster
Debbie Doom, El Monte
Nancy Evans, Glendale
Lisa Fernandez, Long Beach
Stephanie Fleischaker, Huntington Beach
Gina Givogri, Elk Grove
Sara Griffin, Simi Valley
Michelle Gromacki, Antioch
Yvonne Gutierrez, Los Angeles
Kelley Jackson, Citrus Heights
Alison Johnsen, Irvine
Barbara Jordan, Huntington Beach
Nina Lindenberg, Anaheim Hills
Kim Maher, Fresno
Sara Mallett, Whittier
Stacey Nuveman, LaVerne
Leah O'Brien, Chino
Cyndi Parrus, Covina
Priscilla Rouse, Lakeview Terrace
Christa Saindon, Cerritos
Julie Smith, Glendora
Lidia Stiglich, Albany
Shelly Stokes, Carmichael

Karen Walker-Deegan, Woodland Hills
Dee Dee Weiman, Los Angeles

CONNECTICUT:
Pat Dufficy, Stratford

DELAWARE:
Dionna Harris, Wilmington

FLORIDA:
Dot Richardson, Orlando

ILLINOIS:
Holly Aprile, Charleston
Jill Justin, Oak Lawn
Missy Nowak, Chicago

INDIANA:
Michelle Venturella, Bloomington

IOWA:
Beth Kirchner, Sioux City
Dani Tyler, Des Moines
Cathy Wylie, Ames

MICHIGAN:
Patti Benedict, Wyoming
Bonnie Tholl, Ann Arbor

MINNESOTA:
Jenny Condon, Edina

MISSOURI:
Kacey Marshall, Columbia
Kellyn Tate, Chesterfield

NEVADA:
Lori Harrigan, Las Vegas
Martha O'Kelley, Las Vegas

NEW JERSEY:
Trish Popowski, Laurence Harbor
Michele Smith, Califon

PENNSYLVANIA:
Jackie Cipolloni, Philadelphia
Eileen Schmidt, Barto

SOUTH CAROLINA:
Karen Sanchelli, Columbia

TENNESSEE:
Cheri Kempf, Brentwood

TEXAS:
Nikki Cockrell, Pasadena
Jennifer McFalls, Grand Prairie
Christa Williams, Houston

ABOVE (CLOCKWISE, FROM TOP RIGHT):
Level I Tryouts at Long Beach City College, California; Peak Camp at Long Beach City College, California; Level I Tryouts at Marietta, Georgia; Level I Tryouts at Springfield, Massachusetts; Level I Tryouts at Ohio State University; Level I Tryouts at Phoenix, Arizona; Level I Tryouts at Lawrence, Kansas; Level I Tryouts at Ft. Worth, Texas.

Photos courtesy of USA Softball.

I ISF JUNIOR WOMEN'S WORLD CHAMPIONSHIP

July 5-12, 1981 Edmonton, Alberta, Canada

USA TEAM *Silver Medalists*
Ron Clarke, head coach
Rich Spiekerman, assistant coach
Jeri Clarke, assistant coach
Jeannette Beemer
Tami Clarke
Tracy Compton
Lisa Norman
Lisa Ishikawa
Diane Dyckma
Rhonda Pittman
Melissa Jansen
Jeanette Burke
Chris Roybal
Kari Johnson
Robin Steman
Becky Suttmann
Barby Suttmann
Iva Jackson
Kandy Foust
Tawny Kanae

II ISF JUNIOR WOMEN'S WORLD CHAMPIONSHIP

July 5-13, 1985 Fargo, North Dakota

USA TEAM *Bronze Medalists*
Phil Bruder, manager
Colleen Silva, assistant manager
Michele Granger
Yvette Baltazar
Nina Ochoa
Lorie Fausett
Stephanie Miller
Valerie Van Kirk
Kelli Flaczinski
Ellen Castro
Michelle Phillips
Jody Schwartz
Samanta Ford
Karyn Rice
Martha Noffsinger (O'Kelley)
Liz Mizera
Jennifer Allard
Yvonne Gutierrez
Lisa Cannon

BELOW: *1987 ISF Junior Women's World Champions.*
Photo Courtesy of USA Softball.

III ISF JUNIOR WOMEN'S WORLD CHAMPIONSHIP

July 10-18, 1987 Oklahoma City, Oklahoma

USA TEAM *Gold Medalists*
John Gregg, coach
John Longaker, coach
Fred Illsley, coach
Jennifer Allard
Susan Bradach
Christy Brown
Angela Clement
Melissa Coombes
Cynthia Demetriff
Michele Granger
Lori Gregg
Yvette Hernandez
Carey Hess
Heather Illsley
Lorraine Maynez
Marian Mendoza
Karyn Rice
Julie Smith
Patti Taylor
Erica Ziencina

IV ISF JUNIOR WOMEN'S WORLD CHAMPIONSHIP

April 20-27, 1991 Adelaide, Australia

USA TEAM *Silver Medalists*
Larry Mays, coach
Ron Clarke, assistant coach
Lynette Bird
Maureen Brady
Jennifer Brewster
Michelle Collins
Laura Espinoza
Kathy Evans
Erika Grogg
Melissa Jantz
Stephanie Keeler
Melinda Mapp
Mieko Nagata
Ramona Nard
Brandi Phillips

Marla Pickard
Katherine Stahl
Nicole Turley
Cyndi Parus

V ISF JUNIOR WOMEN'S WORLD CHAMPIONSHIP

June 24-July 1, 1995 Normal, Illinois

USA TEAM *Gold Medalists*
Margie Wright, head coach
Diane Schumacher, assistant coach
Gary Haning, assistant coach
Julie Adams
Christie Ambrosi
Shannon Beeler
Nikki Cockrell
Lindsey Collins
Courtney Dale
Jamie Graves
Kim Gutridge
Nina Lindenberg
Toni Mascarenas
Brandee McArthur
Stacey Nuveman
Lori Reese
Christa Saindon
Amanda Scott
Kellie Wiginton
Christa Williams

BELOW: *1995 ISF Junior Women's World Champions.*
Photo Courtesy of USA Softball.

USA UMPIRES AT THE WOMEN'S WORLD AND PAN AMERICAN GAMES CHAMPIONSHIPS

1965 World: Bob McClay

1970 World: Rex Brown

1974 World: Merle Butler, Paul Brown, Mel Neece and Dick Alexander

1978 World: Don Olson and Jerry Kenney

1979 Pan Am: Jimmy Fannon and Harry Trimm

1981 Jr. World: Rex Brown

1982 World: Morrie Olsen

1983 Pan Am: Henry Flowers and Danny Rhodes

1985 Jr. World: Ron Ballantyne, Lyle Joe McWilliams, Kevin Morrison and Jack Sauder

1986 World: Johnny Welton

1987 Pan Am: Jack Futeron, Larry Hood, Julie Johnson, Ken Kendall, Lyle Joe McWilliams, Kevin Morrison, Don Stillwell, Ken Thaxton, Kathy Strahm, Nick Cinquanto, Marie Koch and Ron Welch

1990 World: Edward Crane, Julie Johnson, Penny Knuff, Marie Koch, Kathy Strahm and William Tripp

1991 Pan Am: Curt Moreno and Jeff Hansen

1991 Jr. World: Billy Monk and Sonny Pompilli

1994 World: Marty Makar, Horace Murdock, Robert Scott and Cheryl Simmons

1995 Olympic Qualifier, Harlem, Netherlands, Nick Cinquanto

1995 Olympic Qualifier, Auckland, New Zealand, Cheryl Simmons

1995 Olympic Qualifier, San Juan, Puerto Rico, Robert Scott and Cheryl Simmons

1995 Pan Am: Emily Alexander and Nick Finck

1995 Jr. World: Bonnie Anderson, Michael Bessner, Craig Cress, Cheryl Klug, Hank Koritkoski and Lola Wheeler

1996 Olympic Games: Emily Alexander, Julie Johnson, Kathy Strahm and Jeff Hansen